YOUR BEST ROCKIN' LIFE
PHOTOGRAPHER

A Signature Career Book
Series for Teens

BY **DENISE READ**

"Photography is a way of feeling, of touching, of loving. What you have caught on film is captured forever... **It remembers little things, long after you have forgotten everything.**"

—Aaron Siskind

Your Best Rockin' Life
Photographer
A Signature Career Book Series
by Denise Read

Copyright © 2024 by Rock Your Life Media, LLC

All Rights Reserved. No part of this publication may be reproduced, distributed, or transmitted in any form or by any means, including photocopying, without the prior written permission of the publisher, except in the case of brief quotations embodied in critical reviews and certain other noncommercial uses permitted by copyright law.

Published by: Rock Your Life Media, LLC

www.rockyourlifemedia.com

Cover Design: Rock Your Life Media, LLC

Cover Photo Credit: Tim Sabatino

Interior Design: Justin Oefelein

Photo Enhancements: Adobe Stock Photo

ISBN Print   979-8-9911079-2-1

ISBN Digital   979-8-9911079-3-8

Printed in the United States of America

For permissions requests, please email denise@rockyourlifemedia.com.

Your Best Rockin' Life

TABLE OF CONTENTS*

(*see definition at the bottom of this page)

PHOTOGRAPHER

Author's Preface	Page 1
Introduction	Page 13
What is Your Purpose in Life	Page 25
Chapter 1 – Definition and History of Photography	Page 37
Chapter 2 – The Purpose of a Photographer	Page 51
Chapter 3 – Career Basics	Page 63
Chapter 4 – Some Career Possibilities	Page 75
Chapter 5 – Training and Getting a Job	Page 87
Chapter 6 – Meet Professional Photographers	Page 103
In Closing	Page 121
Glossary	Page 125

*This symbol is an asterisk. It means there is a reference to this item somewhere else, usually at the bottom of the same page. This asterisk (in blue) informs you that all words in **BOLD BLUE** are in the glossary at the back of this book.

You are what you think about.
If you believe it, IT IS SO.
— UNKNOWN

Your Best Rockin' Life

Author's Preface*

*Author's preface is an introductory statement from the author, setting forth the purpose and main ideas of a book.

Would you BELIEVE...

If I told you right now that you can have ANYTHING in the world you want…. Would you believe me? You might not, and that's ok. But I want you to think for a minute and write down a few things you'd like to have. I'll start. Here are a few of mine…

- A big house (a mansion) with a pool.
- A million dollars, and more coming every year.
- Trips around the world to wonderful and exotic places.
- Teenagers that are excited about their future and learning about careers.

Ok, your turn…

1. _____

2. _____

3. _____

4. _____

Think of something recently you wanted. It could've been to see a friend, get a new game or just have a cookie. What was the first thing you did when you decided that you wanted that thing? Probably you asked for it or just went ahead and did it, right? Because even a little kid knows that you're probably not going to have someone come along and just give you whatever you are thinking about. If you ask for a cookie, there's a much better chance you'll get it than if you just sit there thinking about it.

Did you ever want something so badly that you did chores and saved up your own money to buy it? It might have looked like this:

- Decided you wanted something and named it.
    - "I want a new skateboard."
- Picked out the skateboard so you knew exactly what it looked like, where you would buy it and how much it cost.
- Pictured yourself riding the skateboard, going to the skate park, doing tricks.
- Talked to your mom or dad to see if they'd help you buy it or take you to the store when you had the money.
- Decided how you would get the money. Maybe you had some savings, maybe not. If not, you worked out what you would need to do to earn the money, and how long it would take.
- Continued to hold the vision of having the skateboard, feeling very thankful that it was about to be yours.
- Did the work and got the money.
- Took the money to the store and bought it.
- Goal achieved.

This cycle is the exact same, no matter what it is you want, though it's not always a smooth road.

You might change your mind halfway through and decide you want a video game instead. Then, later you want the skateboard again. Or not. It's ok to change your mind or change direction.

Typically, the bigger the goal, the longer it takes because there will be more work to do to get there – though not always. You could want something so bad, and your vision so strong that you are willing to work harder and faster, and you will achieve it sooner.

If you want to be a doctor, for example, you don't just decide and be a doctor starting today. You need to finish high school, finish college and then finish medical school. However, there are things you can do today to be a doctor. More about that below.

SUPER BIG GOAL
= More Work To Get It
= Might Take Longer To Achieve

Dreamers create things. People that believe in themselves are the ones that get what they want. Do you know someone that has a dream, even though they never told you what the dream was? The girl that loves going to her dance classes, or the boy who can't wait to get back into the science lab are showing their goals without talking about them. They know what they want. They have decided, and they are doing the work.

Do people with definite goals always have good days? Are they always happy and thrilled to do the work? Probably not. But they do it anyway. Why? Because they have a dream, and they want to achieve it more than they want to give it up. Failures will happen. And you will make mistakes along the way. Keep your goal in mind and continue to see yourself achieving it. Live it in your mind. Many times, failures mean there is something even better coming. Mistakes are there to tell you to do something different. Yesterday is gone. Five minutes ago is gone. When you do something you regret, forgive yourself immediately and move on *knowing* that good things are coming your way!

> "Day by day, in every way, I am getting better and better."
> —Émile Coué

Think of something in your life that you decided you wanted and then got it. How did you do it? Well, the first step was to believe you could have it, right? And then you probably kept it in your mind and thought about it a lot. You pictured having it. You probably had to do some work for it, even if was doing some chores to earn money. If you had to save money you probably didn't buy other things because you wanted to keep all your money for this one thing.

Think back to being a doctor. Yes, you need many years of school to be a doctor, but do you necessarily have to wait until you are fully out of school to be a doctor? Yes and no. Yes, in order to be an actual medical doctor, you do need a medical degree to start treating patients. BUT… you can always start your career by helping out in a doctor's office, either as an intern or a volunteer, to watch and learn.

If you want to be a pro baseball player, you can try to be a bat boy for a college or pro team while you're in school. What an amazing way to learn about being a baseball player! You don't need to be a certain age or have a special skill to start doing what you want. All you need is to believe, keep a positive attitude, do things concerning it and talk about what you want to those that can help you. Somewhere along the way, an opportunity is sure to pop up if you believe it will.

 *If you believe it, you can achieve it.*

Getting what you want is not easy. You can't just think your way into winning the lottery or being a star athlete. But you can train your mind to believe you can have what you want, and then know you will do whatever it takes to get it. If you don't want to do whatever it takes to have something, I wouldn't think you wanted it that bad. Would you?

Go back to the goals you wrote above. Do you want to change any of them, maybe make them bigger? Many times, thinking big, REALLY BIG, is the only way you can motivate yourself to DO WHATEVER IT TAKES to succeed.

Do you believe in magic? Miracles? Are you a dreamer? One thing I have learned, because I've seen it and I've done it myself, is that when you believe in miracles, miracles happen. When you allow yourself big, wonderful dreams, you are happy and excited to pursue them.

I'll give you an example. Let's say you don't think you can achieve a really big goal, so you have a small goal. Say you are a football player, and you want to win the championship. That's a big goal, right?

You say, "But, I can't win a football championship all by myself, no matter how much I want it or believe I can do it." Yes, that's true. But don't make your goal smaller just because you are only one person. Take it one step further. Keep your dream big. Work to be the best player you can possibly be. Ask your coach to help you. Talk to your teammates about winning the championship and get them excited so they want to work hard too. See? You are just one person, but you can make a difference for a whole team and help win the championship for everyone.

Preface

You are not "just one little person". You are one BIG PERSON and you have the power to motivate everyone else around you to help… or get them to jump out of the way when they are in the way!

Nothing is free and nothing worthwhile comes easy. If you think you don't need to do anything to achieve your goals, you might as well stop reading this right now. How do think Olympic athletes get their chance? Not just because they wanted it and believed in themselves and had faith. What else did they need to do? (Key word – DO) Work for it, of course! They needed to train, which for an Olympic athlete usually means many, many years of hard work. I bet if you asked an Olympian if it was worth it, he'd say yes because that was his goal.

Would you do it? Do you want to be in the Olympics and work your butt off for many years to get there? You might and you might not. Would you like to invent new electronics or computer apps? Think about what you want, but also what you don't want. For me, I don't want to be a world class chef and open my own restaurant. I don't want to be a doctor or dentist. I don't want to be a teacher, I don't want to be a fireman, and I really don't want to be a police officer. I don't want to be a nurse, office manager, painter, photographer, politician, graphic designer, pilot, barber, scientist, or plumber. These things you don't want to do are just as important as things you do want to do.

Can you see how there are SO MANY THINGS to do and SO MANY WAYS to stand out as an original?

Ok, back to your goal. Once you've named it, and you truly have faith that you can and will achieve it, figure out the actions you need to take to get it. To be an Olympic swimmer, you need to spend a lot of time in the pool. In addition to that, you'll need to eat right, get enough sleep, keep a positive attitude, and learn how other swimmers got to the Olympics. Picking the right coach is probably pretty important.

Know what actions will help your journey to success and what actions won't. Watching TV will never help any goal, unless you watch something educational that helps you do the actions better. Playing video games may make you a good competitor, but do you know what it would take to be a world class gamer? Would you be willing to give up all your friends, all your sports, not go on vacation with your family, miss holidays, not play outside, or go to the beach – all because you need to keep playing video games? Would you want to do that? That's like saying it would be great to eat only candy for every meal, but how long would it take to get tired of eating just candy? Not long, I'm sure. Gaming is a very lonely sport, and those that get to the top don't do much of anything else.

Be careful what you wish for.

Preface

> You just might get it.
> —UNKNOWN

To choose a goal, answer these two questions:

1. What do you want more than *anything* else?
2. Would you do *anything* to have it?

I'm sure you have heard that every person has a different fingerprint. Truly, no two people are exactly alike, even identical twins. Just like snowflakes, we are all unique and individual and are not like anyone else in this entire world. You are a one of a kind among over 8 billion people! Wow. That's original!

In your one in 8 billion people uniqueness, you also have one in 8 billion magic within you – magic that is only yours. When you think of the famous gamer or most talented athlete or successful musician, remember that those people have nothing to do with you. They just happened to find their magic and had a dream they worked hard to achieve.

Find YOUR magic and then set a goal so big and so strong that you will do anything to get it!

There are some simple but definite steps you can take to achieve a goal as fast as possible:

1. Have a goal – something you want really bad!
2. Believe in yourself – know, 100% that you have magic in you that no one else has.
3. Have faith you will get it – know you will do whatever it takes, no matter what.
4. Don't talk about your goal, except to those that can help you. Lots of people will be jealous or negative and you can't have any negativity near you – it will definitely slow you down!
5. Be thankful and grateful for everything you have and will have. Always appreciate the road you are on, and everyone and everything that's on it with you.
6. Think only positive thoughts and keep telling yourself that you *will* get there.
7. Work hard and don't do wasteful things. Playing Fortnite isn't going to help you be a better cook, so get back in the kitchen and cook!
8. Repeat. Repeat. Repeat.

Preface

The last step is key to it all. How does a baby learn to walk? They don't take a couple of steps, give up, and then never walk. No matter how long it takes, babies keep trying to walk until they walk. So, until you become a famous race car driver, you need to keep repeating all the steps above, over and over, until you get there. Think about your goal, believe in yourself, know you have magic and be certain you will get there. Make sure to be thankful for the road you are on because it's the right road, and since it's the right road, you will surely arrive – as long as you keep moving forward. Work hard for your goal. Over and over, and over and over again.

Come back and reread this chapter anytime you need a lift.

There is no one like you and no one can do what you can do. I believe in you. If you believe in you and you have big dreams within you, this book series is for you.

Preface Chapter Questions

1. List a couple things that you have gotten or achieved because you believed you could.

2. Write down several good things about yourself that make you different from other people you know.

3. Name at least one thing you want when you get older that you know you will get.

4. Pick out a couple people you know and write what you think their goals are based on what you see them doing.

Your Best Rockin' Life

Introduction

> "Success is no accident. It is hard work, perseverance, learning, studying, sacrifice, and most of all, love of what you are doing or learning to do."
> —Pelé

"What do you want to be when you grow up?"

How many people have asked you that question? What was your answer?

I think the question should be, "What do you want to *do* when you grow up?" Isn't working *doing*? If you were an airline pilot, how would you think it would work to sit in that cockpit and "be" a pilot? Even if you have the uniform, the pilot's hat, and the wings pinned to your shirt, that plane will not fly anywhere unless you DO something about it!

As I see it, you *become* the pilot, photographer, attorney, writer, or YouTuber after you *do* the work. First, you need to learn about it. What does a video game creator do? Create video games, right? Ok, so the guy *does the work to* create and develop video games. Learn what it takes to do the job and then do it. Pretty simple.

A house painter needs to have paint and brushes and possibly a ladder or other tools and understand how to paint a house without painting the windows, bushes, and grass. If someone wanted to be a house painter, he would have to have all that *basic information*, what kinds of paint are best for different houses and what brushes to use on certain parts of the house. You get the idea. Once you have all the essential data about doing a job, you will want to have all the tools close by, and then you will *do* the job repeatedly until you can do it better than anyone else. The better you are at a job, the more you will be paid to do it.

Make sense?

Think of some things you do. Do you play any sports? Chess? An instrument? Video games? You *do* homework, right? Your mom probably has you *doing* chores around the house. You must shower, brush your teeth, put your shoes on, and so on. So, it is clear. You DO a lot of stuff every day.

Now, think about some things you do well. Not necessarily something you like to do, but stuff you do well. Think back to the first few times you were doing those things. Were you good at it the very first time you did it? Even walking, which you probably do perfectly now, did not just happen. You had to learn how to move your legs, one in front of the other, and balance to move forward! No matter what you are good at, the more you do it, the better you get. It is a lot more fun if you also like doing it, but that is not as important as understanding this:

If you keep doing something over and over, you will get better.

Guaranteed.

For example, if your mom likes it when you make your bed every morning, you will get better and faster at it, even if you do not like it.

Do you see that you can learn anything you want (in the whole world!) and get to the point where you are doing it expertly? It is good to remember this because you will be learning for the rest of your life. You will get better at every action you do repetitively. This fact should make you feel excited about doing things you want.

When I was in high school, I played the clarinet. Someday I want to learn how to play the flute. I have a flute, so I will take lessons or dive into an online class when the time is right for me. Then I will practice to get better.

The time you spend getting better at something depends on your natural talent and determination. If you have a natural talent, you will get better faster. You can still learn anything you want if you do not have a natural talent. When you are determined to do something, you will practice until you are great.

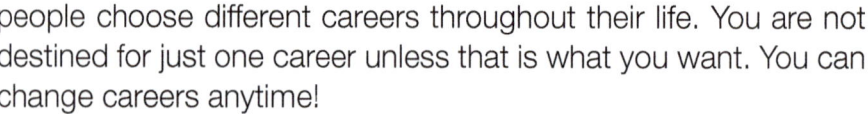

Your career is something you choose to do practically every day for pretty much the rest of your life. Sounds important, doesn't it? It can be a huge decision, especially if you need a lot of training to get there. Doctors need to go to school for many years, even after college. However, many people choose different careers throughout their life. You are not destined for just one career unless that is what you want. You can change careers anytime!

Think of something you love doing so much you "get lost" in it. I like writing. I also get lost in setting small goals for myself and completing them – reading a chapter in a book I am studying, running six miles, finishing my laundry (!!). I also get lost in learning something new or spending time with my family and friends. If you know what you get lost in, you only need to figure out how to get someone to pay you for it. That is a career you will be happy to have for a long time!

When you do something you love, you *become* the person that does that. Read that sentence again and let it sink in. The airplane pilot can now *be* a pilot because he has learned and practiced everything he needs to do and has gotten good at it. He puts on his uniform, his pilot's hat, and wings and can go to the airport, walk directly to a plane, and get in the cockpit. He looks like a pilot. He is *being* a pilot, so others believe he is a pilot. See how *being* something and *doing* it are different, but related?

The other thing to consider is what you want to *have* from your work.

Millions of dollars? The satisfaction of healing sick people? Fame? A happy family? Your name in magazines or your songs on the radio?

Knowing what you want to have will help lead you to things you can do to have those things. If money is your goal, you might not want to work at the fast-food drive-up window for the rest of your life. If a family is what you want to have, maybe you will want to do a job where you can work at home and be with your family.

See how these fit together: have, do, and be? If you figure out what you want to *have*, you can determine what you need to *do* to have that and then *be* the person who does those things.

I am super excited you are reading this book!

The purpose of this book and the entire *Your Best Rockin' Life* series is to provide basic information that is easy to understand for someone wanting to learn more about a career.

This book will provide information and examples about a career's different parts to better understand it. You will learn about its history, why people do it, what kind of people do it, similar jobs, what kind of training you will need, and where to get it. You will also meet professionals with tips for how to do it successfully.

After each chapter, answer a few questions to test your understanding. Do not skip these! Doing these exercises and answering the questions will help you think of yourself in this career and how it might be a good fit for *your future*. Or not.

My goal for you in reading this book is that you will learn something new about yourself, even if it is deciding that this career is not for you. In this series, each book focuses on a different career. I want you to think about what job would make you excited to do when you get older – something you would like to get started on now! I want to inspire you to be the best, happiest, most successful YOU. You are in charge of your life and can do anything you want – do not let anyone tell you any different!

Make sure to keep a dictionary handy and stop and look up the definitions for any words you are not 100% certain you understand. Understanding definitions will broaden your vocabulary and make it easier to learn things in the future. Words in **bold blue** are in the glossary. In school, you might try to find the meaning of a word by its "context." Be careful with this! You might find something "makes sense" in context but the wrong meaning for the word! It only takes a moment to look up words that are not instantly 100% clear to you. You will be thankful you did, and you will learn faster.

Do you ever have problems studying?

A few things can happen when you study something new that may lead you *away* from the subject instead of toward it. Please pay attention to the following manifestations, as they warn you about problems in your study, causing you not to want to study the subject. I include a warning sign of a study problem and how to handle it to get back on track with your study of this book. Remember this and use it when you are studying anything new.

Do you ever get frustrated when you study?

If you are studying something you love but suddenly find yourself uninterested in it or are irritated, ask yourself if you are reading too many words and do not have enough "things" to touch or look at within your study. Goalbook is a company that provides tools to educators to help break through problems in study. In their "Toolkit," they talk about finding things to use, called Literacy **Manipulatives**, to help you understand the subject better. These manipulatives are things you can manipulate (touch, use or look at) and help when the study material does not come with pieces or pictures that show you.

For example, if you are learning how to make ice cream, you will want to see pictures of the tools and ingredients you'll need to make it, and the delicious ice cream you will eat when you finish making it. It will be more enjoyable to learn how to make it when you see pictures of the measuring cups you will use and the ingredients. You will be much more excited to make the ice cream when you can look at or touch the milk you will use, the sugar, the ice, and the bucket you will make it in. You will stay interested and excited until you taste your yummy creation if you have something to look at or touch while learning.

If you read a recipe in a cookbook without pictures, you could get bored and give up before you even start. You might not know what kind of bucket you need to use to make ice cream, or how you use the bucket once you put the ingredients in it. You want something to touch and feel during your study – or at the very least, pictures. If these pictures or tools do not come with your study materials, you can find them yourself by doing an internet search or finding another book. Or grab a notepad and sketch it or use some little things to "manipulate" how it works.

When you sketch it, you just draw a picture of how it's described so you can "see" it. You would do the same with items to "manipulate" it. For example, you could take the "A" in the below picture and say that is the bucket for the ice cream. "O" and "U" are some of the ingredients, "E" is the ice and "I" is the handle on the bucket you need to turn to churn the ice cream. You can "show" how the whole process works by putting these items into the right order according to the directions. Make sense?

Finding a way to see it or do it can help if you feel you are missing something in your reading.

You can use items and manipulate them to understand something better.

Do you ever feel confused when you study?

If you are flying through your study and suddenly find yourself confused, you are likely moving too quickly and missing important information or steps. Slow down and make sure you understand every step.

I bet you can think about a time you were in school where the class was moving along in learning something, maybe math or writing, where you understood the first part, and then suddenly it all became so confusing. You can probably see that the teacher went through the lesson, from beginning to end, but somehow it was just too fast for you.

Students learn things differently and at different speeds. There is no right speed. The time to learn something varies by person. Stop and think about some examples. When you understand that study speed varies, you will notice when you try to go too fast so you can stop and fix it yourself or help someone else.

When you are confused while you study, you are likely trying to learn it too fast. Slow down. Start from where you fully understood it and move forward from there. There is nothing wrong with taking a little more time to ensure you get it. Everyone is different, so remember not to compare yourself to how fast others are going. Encourage others to take more time on confusing subjects and take that advice yourself.

Expand your vocabulary by looking up more words.

If something does not seem crystal clear while studying, it might mean something has a different meaning than you think. You might not have a clear picture of what you are learning if you try to understand it by its context. If you skip over it, you could miss part of the subject. Not understanding every word might not matter if you are reading a novel for pleasure, but it could matter if you need to know something complicated for your job.

One clue that you are skipping over words is that you start feeling like you do not want to study anymore, or you get sleepy or bored.

Make sure you have a good dictionary to look up words quickly when you need to, which is at your level of education. Dictionary.com is fine if the definitions do not cause further confusion. A good student dictionary will also work.

To further build up your vocabulary, look at all of a word's definitions in the dictionary so you will recognize it in anything you read even if it's used in different ways.

You can learn anything you want! If you have any trouble studying, please contact us (www.rockyourlifemedia.com). We would like to help.

EXERCISE

Tayler acted crazy anytime he got a little lucre.

Did you stop at the last word? Do you know what it means?

Below is an example definition of 'lucre' from the Merriam-Webster online dictionary.

lucre

noun (part of speech)

lu·cre | \ lü-kər \
(Pronunciation. Look in the first part of a dictionary to see how to pronounce correctly.)

**Definition of *lucre*
monetary gain, profit**
also: **MONEY**

Synonyms (words that have similar meanings):

bread [*slang*],

bucks,

cabbage [*slang*],

cash,

change,

chips,

coin,

currency,

dough,

gold,

green,

jack [*slang*],

kale [*slang*],

legal tender,

long green [*slang*],

loot,

money,

moola (or moolah) [*slang*],

scratch [*slang*],

shekels,

tender,

wampum

ORIGIN OF Lucre - Middle English, Anglo-French, Latin *lucrum*; probably akin to Old English lēan reward, Old High German lōn, Greek apo*lauein* to enjoy

- Does the sentence make more sense after you read the dictionary definition?
- Did you learn some new words for "money" from the synonyms?
- Did you take the time to read the origin of the word? Did it further help your understanding?
- Do you feel like you added any new words to your vocabulary?

This book and the series aim to give you essential career information to decide if you want to learn more. My vision for you is to be excited about your future. I want you to know what it is like to go to work doing something you love. I want you to learn about many different careers and then have the confidence to chase after your dream job!

I wish only the best of success for you and your future. In reading this book, if you find this is not your career, no problem! Congratulations on learning something new and pick up another *Your Best Rockin' Life* career book.

Here is to your success and your future! Go after what you want! I believe in you.

Introduction Chapter Questions

1. What are study "manipulatives," and when would you use them?

2. If you get confused when you study, should you return and ensure you did not miss any steps or give up?

3. When should you define words by their context? (I will help you with this one: NEVER!) What should you do instead?

4. How will you use this introduction's information in reading this book and series?

• •

Your Best Rockin' Life

What is your Purpose in Life?

(Or – what is it that you are <u>really</u> trying to do?)

> People don't buy what you do. They buy why you do it.
> —Simon Sinek

What is your purpose in life? This is an interesting question. Stop for a moment and think about it.

Definition of Purpose:

1. What you want to get. Your goal.
2. The reason why you do something.

Both of these definitions work for your purpose. It is **WHAT** you want to achieve, and **WHY** you want to achieve it. Do you see the difference? One is what you want to have when your work is done – the desired, final result. The other is why you want that result – the reason you are doing it. Here are some examples:

- Fireman
    - What – Safe environments, and unsafe environments (areas on fire) quickly made safe again.
    - Why – Neighborhoods and cities protected from fires so people can live there safely and happily.
- Restaurant Owner
    - What – Delicious food and drinks delivered to customers quickly and cheerfully.
    - Why – Desire to give people an amazing eating experience that makes them happy.
- Sales Manager
    - What – Lots of sales from hard-working salespeople.
    - Why – To grow the company and be the best in its industry.
- Fashion Designer
    - What – Stylish clothing being worn around the world.
    - Why – To create confidence in people by providing them clothing they feel wonderful, stylish, unique and happy wearing.
- Real Estate Agent
    - What – Houses sold.
    - Why – Helping individuals and families find and buy their dream home and sell their current house for the best price.

What is your Purpose in Life?

The purpose of this book is to give you information about a career category, and some tools to start on the pathway to a career you will be happy with.

- What – a book jam-packed with information about careers.
- Why – To inspire teens to get excited about their life after high school.

Can you think of some other examples?

<u>Purpose is your **reason** for doing the actions needed to **make your goal.**</u> Your WHY. Why do kids need to go to school? Well, the purpose of school is to teach you things you can use in your life. Some people think school is a place to park kids while parents are at work. What happens to kids who do well in school once they start looking for jobs? They find and get good jobs they can be excited about. Right? And, if they work hard and treat others well, they can find really good jobs and make more and more money every year and have fun while they are working.

Your purpose in life is the reason for your life. A friend of mine says her purpose in life is to teach, to help others learn. She loves nothing more than working with kids and seeing their faces light up when they gain a better understanding about something. Do you know what your Mom or Dad's life purpose is? If not, ask them. Remember that purposes can change at different stages of life.

Many times, a purpose has in it something big, like helping people, teaching people, or showing people. The best purposes give you a feeling of duty, like "I have to do this." Actors and singers commonly say this. The entertainment industry is a very competitive and challenging career. Only the very best in these fields will rise to the top, and many times it's those that are driven with a feeling they don't have another choice. Nothing else will make them happy. Some doctors, firefighters, athletes, teachers, coaches, and artists say they knew what they wanted to do from a very young age.

Think of a time when you were young. What did you enjoy? What did you want to be when you grew up? Do you still feel that way?

There are many careers that aren't as well-known as those mentioned above. **Machine operators**, **marketing and advertising professionals**, **salespeople**, **public relations executives**, **graphic designers**, **attorneys**, **auto mechanics** or **caterers**? There are an almost unlimited number of careers, and many careers have careers within them. Sports, for example. We all know about athletes, but there are careers in sports that have nothing to do with being an athlete. **Sports medicine specialist**, **sports agent**, **athletic trainer**, **broadcast journalist**, and **sports photographer** are just a few.

To find your purpose in life, you really need to look closely at yourself. Do you understand yourself? What are you good at? What comes easy for you? What do others tell you you're good at? What do you enjoy doing that you could keep doing for hours? What do you hate doing? What are you bad at, and don't enjoy? We are all different. Something one person may love, another may completely dislike. Think of an example of this in your life. Do you know someone that seems to like or enjoy something that you don't? Do you like talking to others, or spending time alone? Is it easy for you to talk to others, or in front of a group, or not?

Let's dive in.

Personality

Personality traits are the different qualities of someone. It's all the parts of you that make you YOU. These are parts of you that make you different than anyone else. Read the below list of some personality traits. Circle some you feel you have.

Active
Adventurous
Ambitious
Appreciative
Assertive
Athletic
Calm
Capable
Caring
Charming
Cheerful
Clean
Confident
Considerate
Cooperative
Courageous
Creative
Curious
Decisive
Disciplined
Easy to talk to
Efficient
Empathetic
Energetic
Fair

Faithful
Focused
Forceful
Forgiving
Friendly, Likeable
Generous
Gentle
Gets along well with others
Good-natured
Hardworking
Healthy
Helpful
Honest
Humble
Humorous
Imaginative
Independent
Kind
Logical
Lovable
Loyal
Observant
Organized
Patient

Persuasive
Playful
Positive
Powerful
Practical
Relaxed
Reliable
Resourceful
Respectful
Responsible
Secure
Selfless
Self-sufficient
Sensitive
Smart
Sociable
Speaks well
Spontaneous
Stable
Strong
Studious
Tenacious
Trusting
Understanding

Talents

Talents are those things you are good at. They are not necessarily things you enjoy, or even like. But you're good at them.

The good thing about talents and skills is that you have them naturally, like being a good athlete or a good problem-solver, but if you enjoy something, like playing an instrument or skateboarding, you can decide to become better at it and then practice it over and over until it becomes one of your best talents or skills.

It's important to know the difference – what you are good at (whether you like it or not) – and what you would like to be better at.

Below are some talents and skills. Find a few you are naturally good at and circle them.

Ability to focus
Ability to handle Change
Ability to make Friends
Academics
Adaptable
Art - drawing, painting, etc.
Athleticism
Communication Skills
Computers / IT
Creativity
Decision Making
Foreign Language
Health / Fitness
Helping others get along with each other
Imaginative
Inventive
Jokes / Humor
Leadership
Managing Time
Math – Managing Money
Music, singing, playing an instrument
Not easily disappointed
Photography
Problem Solving
Public Speaking
Raising Money
Research
Sign Language
Software
Telling or Creating Stories
Teaching / Training
Typing
Creating Videos
Woodworking
Writing

Do you have some personality traits and natural talents and skills circled? Did you pick out a few things you'd like to be better at? If not, do that now. Maybe you'd like to be more outgoing or more organized. Perhaps you'd like to be better at photography or public speaking.

If you put your personality and talents together with the reason (your purpose) for your work, you will be well on your way to finding your perfect career. The reason why these three together can provide the best career choice is simple. Think of a guy. This guy loves animals, has patience and enjoys helping. His talents include not being grossed out by blood, understanding complicated things and being able to solve complicated problems quickly. He feels it's his duty to help make ill or injured animals well again. What do you think the natural career choice would be for him? You got it: a veterinarian.

Or, how about a girl who is super fun to be around, very friendly, sweet, and passionate. These are some of her personality traits. She loves fashion and spends her free time coordinating colors and styles of her clothes and shoes. She loves helping her friends with their clothing choices. She is creative and extremely imaginative. Can you guess what career she might like? How about a fashion designer?

I'm not going to lie to you. It's not always easy to put all these things together and come up with a career "just like that". That being said, know that these three – talents, personality and purpose – when they all line up, will give you unstoppable energy and a passion for your life. You will love getting up every day to go to work. On the other hand, if you get a job you're good at (have talent for), but don't have the personality or purpose for it, you may end up disappointed. If you're great at fixing computers but hate to work alone and love being active outdoors, you will likely not be happy in a job where you sit alone fixing computers all day. Maybe this would be a great weekend job, or something you do every now and then for fun, but as a career? Likely not.

If one's personality is friendly and he loves talking to people, and has a purpose to inspire others, and a talent for speaking foreign languages, he could get a job as a translator. But… do you think he would be happy translating if his purpose is to inspire others? Maybe or maybe not. He could also get a job as a motivational speaker where he travels the world using his foreign languages to inspire others. If he doesn't like being in the spotlight, he could partner with a motivational speaker and translate their speeches into other languages. There are many ways to create the perfect career fit for you.

Take the talents and skills list and decide how you are going to get better at some of these things. What would you need to do to improve? If you want to be more outgoing, you might get involved in groups at school or at your church or with your friends, where you need to talk to people. To get better at photography, you could set aside 20 minutes a day, or a couple hours on the weekend and use it only to learn more about photography and taking pictures.

You can do this for anything you are interested in, whether or not it's listed here. Think of things that are exciting to you, things that you love learning about or doing. This will give you clues into what might (or might not) be a good career for you. If you find that you have a hard time sitting still for long periods of time, a career in front of a computer screen will likely not sound good to you. Likewise, if you determine that sports are your favorite thing, but being a professional athlete isn't appealing to you, you can look for other careers in the athletic industry that you would like to pursue based on your other personality traits, skills and talents.

No matter where you start from, just starting is the key. If you have a purpose for your life, and you have some idea of your natural talents and skills, and know what you'd like to develop, get going! Pick up a *Your Best Rockin' Life* career book and see where it takes you. You can always change your mind or change direction. If you can't find what you are looking for in one of our books, please email us so we can create a book for you.

Here is to your future success!

If you can dream it, you can do it.

—Walt Disney

Purpose Chapter Questions

1. What does it mean to have a Life Purpose?

2. Think of a career that isn't listed above. What is the purpose of that career: the WHAT, and the WHY?

3. Write down three things you want to develop, whether they are personality traits or talents and skills. Now, write down three things you can do for each one to get better at them.

4. Based on the above, what do think your Life Purpose is today?

What is your Purpose in Life?

Photographer

Chapter 1

Definition and History of Career

> "No place is boring if you've had a good night's sleep and have a pocket full of **unexposed film**."
> —Robert Adams

What is a Photographer?

A **photographer** (the **Greek** *phos*, meaning "light," and *graphê*, meaning "drawing, writing," together meaning "drawing with light") is a person who takes **photographs**. This word is said to have been created by **Sir John Herschel** in 1839.

Photography is the creative practice of recording images that convey messages for various purposes, including business, communication, advertising, film, art, recreation, or just hobby.

A photographer can be an amateur if he takes pictures for pleasure or fun. An amateur photographer does not intend to sell or make money from his photographs, whereas a **professional** photographer takes pictures to get paid.

A photographer who does photography for a job or career can work for a company, such as a newspaper or advertising agency, or could work freelance, being hired and paid for only one project, like a wedding or other single event.

We are talking about professional photographers in this book.

There are many different types of photographers, so anyone interested in one style can usually do what they like. For example, if you are interested in beauty and fashion, you could be a fashion photographer. Or, if you enjoy animals or the outdoors, you could specialize in those areas and find people who will pay you to take those pictures.

Specialties can be almost endless. You could be an advertising photographer and work for an advertising agency or be a sports photographer if you are really into sports.

Photographers who produce moving pictures (movies or videos) are called **videographers** or **cinematographers**. In a later chapter, we will explore different career specialties.

Remember that making money doing the type of photography you want means continually practicing and getting so good at it that you can sell it to the people who want to buy that type of photography.

The History of Photography

As you read about the history of photography, I suggest you go slowly and ensure you fully understand all its aspects. Some parts can be confusing, but fully understanding how photography started will help you become a highly paid professional.

Compared to some of the oldest careers, like toolmaker (2.6 million years old), hunter (1.8 million years old), and storyteller (200,000 years old), photography is a new profession. In the last 200 years, the camera has developed from a box that recorded light into a blurry image to the super clear and focused pictures a professional can capture with a high-tech digital camera.

Two fundamental discoveries came together to start the process of taking pictures. First, Johannes Kepler discovered camera obscura in the early 1600s. Camera obscura means "darkroom" and happens naturally when an image or scene is projected through a small hole onto a surface on the other side using light. The image was upside down and backward, but otherwise, it was the same.

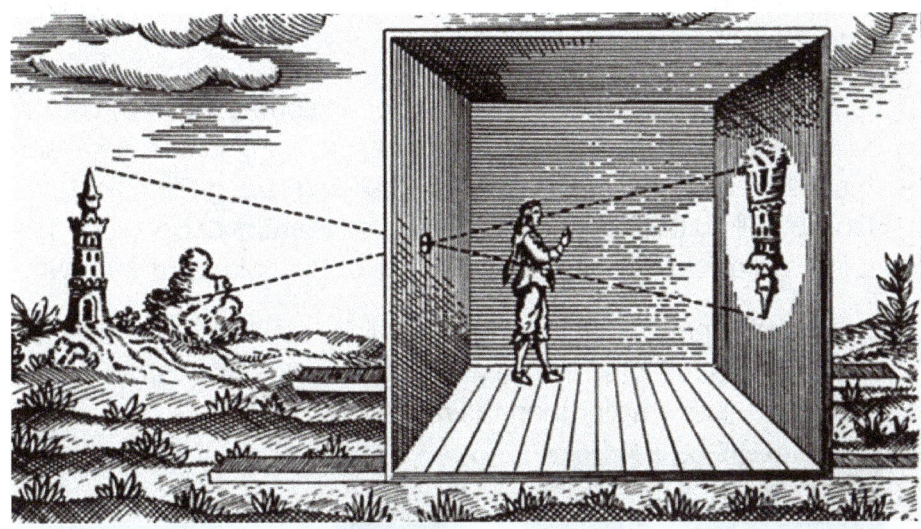

A Camera Obscura. baytrust.org.uk

The second discovery was that certain chemical substances were changed when light hit them. These substances were then used, with light, to create images. However, at this point, there was no way to make these images permanent.

A Chinese philosopher named Mozi wrote about the camera obscura in the 5th century BC. He said that the upside-down image was caused by light traveling in straight lines. When sunshine hits objects that are then reflected into the hole of the camera obscura, the top of the image travels straight down, and the bottom travels straight up. You can see this illustrated in the picture above.

Aristotle, a Greek philosopher, noticed that sunlight passing through gaps in leaves on a tree projected an image of an eclipsed sun on the ground. An eclipse means to be obscured, darkened, or covered up. The sun appeared on the ground because the light passed through the leaves.

Other people worked with the camera obscura for almost two thousand more years before Leonardo da Vinci wrote about it. Leonardo, who lived from 1452 to 1519, is considered one of the most talented people ever. He is known for his paintings and sculptures and is recognized in **science**, **engineering**, **architecture,** and **anatomy.**

Leonardo described it by saying that when something (a place, the outline of a building, or a landscape) has sunlight shining on it, and one drills a small hole in the wall of a building facing the object, the sunlight will go through the hole (called an **aperture** or opening). The object will appear on the opposite wall of the hole, upside-down.

Da Vinci also noted that placing a thin piece of white paper over the upside-down reflected image will show the picture's natural shape and color—just smaller than the real thing.

An example of what a camera obscura image looks like

Although the camera obscura could not record images, it could project upside-down images onto another surface, which someone could outline for artistic creations.

In 1717, in his studies, Johann Heinrich Schulze accidentally found that if he mixed a bit of chalk and nitric acid (a yellowish liquid that is poisonous and made in a laboratory) with dissolved silver particles, it got darker when exposed to sunlight.

Tiphaigne de la Roche wrote a science fiction novel in 1760 that described the development of color pictures. Then, in 1777, Carl Wilhelm Scheele, a chemist, played around with some chemicals and found he could get images to "stick" by using silver chloride. Later, in the 1820s, a guy named Nicephore Niepce also used silver chloride to create permanent images—more on him below.

Around 1800, Thomas Wedgwood, inspired by Scheele, experimented with making pictures that would last. His experiments led to placing objects on light-sensitive material (the first photo paper) and then putting light on it. Exposure is the process of putting light on something. When an object was placed on photo paper and exposed to sunlight, the object's outline remained on the paper after the light was removed.

Back to Nicephore Niepce. In the mid-1820s, he figured out how to fix an image from the first camera. It required at least eight hours and sometimes many days of exposure to light, and the results were not particularly good. He used paper coated with a chemical mixture called silver chloride. He created photographic images in a "negative," meaning an image is the darkest in the lightest areas and lightest in the darkest areas. See the picture of a negative below.

A negative

CHAPTER ONE

The first photographic portrait image of a human ever produced.

"Robert Cornelius, head-and-shoulders [self-] portrait, facing front, with arms crossed," approximate quarter plate daguerreotype, 1839 [Oct of Nov]. LC-USZC4-5001 DLC. Also, see Library of Congress, American Memory, for a complete source description.

Niepce worked alongside a man named Louis Daguerre. When Niepce died in 1833, Daguerre took his notes and created what is today known as the Daguerreotype process. This process only required a few minutes of light exposure in the camera to produce a clear picture.

Daguerre was interested in silver-based photographic processes, so he experimented with taking pictures on a silver plate (like a mirror) with iodine vapor. The iodine (a non-metal substance used in medicine) reacted with the silver to form a silver iodide coating. However, the light exposure took awfully long until Daguerre discovered that mercury (a toxic metal substance used in thermometers to show temperature) fumes could be used during exposure to speed up the process and the picture visibility. A hot solution with common salt secured the image to the paper and removed the excess silver iodide. Exposure times went from hours and days to just minutes.

This silver Daguerreotype process was introduced to the world at the French Academy of Sciences in 1839 and spread quickly. It was used until about 1851 when the collodion process replaced it.

The collodion process, invented by Frederick Scott Archer, also called the "collodion wet plate process," involves putting a wet chemical coating on the material the picture will be on, making it sensitive to light. The image is then exposed to sunlight and developed in about fifteen minutes in a darkroom. The room's darkness helps keep the light away from the developing photographic material.

Color photography was created in 1861 by taking three different photographs, each through a red, green, or blue filter, and then each placed on top of the other using three projectors to project the image. Since it was hard to use light **emulsions** (chemicals used to create sensitivity to light) to make color sensitivity on film when developing, color photography did not progress much further.

Ironically, two French inventors working independently, Louis Ducos du Hauron and Charles Cros, introduced their practically identical ideas about color photography on the same day in 1869. Their method allowed the three color-filtered photographs (red, green, and blue) to be printed on paper, so there was no need to project them to see the color.

Eventually, in the mid-1880s, color emulsions sensitive to all the colors of the spectrum were created.

Using film in photography was created by George Eastman, who made paper film in 1885 and then switched to celluloid in 1888. Celluloid combines chemicals and dyes that set a picture on film. Eastman called his first camera the "Kodak," a simple box camera with a fixed (unmoving) lens and one **shutter speed**. It had enough film for 100 exposures. Once all the pictures were taken, the camera was returned to the company to develop the images and load more film.

The Autochrome plate came next. Brothers Auguste and Louis Lumiere created and introduced it into the marketplace in 1907. Going further than using red, green, and blue color filters, these guys used a "mosaic screen plate" process. A mosaic is a gathering of things, in this case, colors. Dyed red-orange, green, and blue-violet grains of potato starch were the mosaic colors placed on one side of a glass plate. The grains worked as filters that blended the emulsion and exposure to light, allowing all the various shades of the final picture to come through.

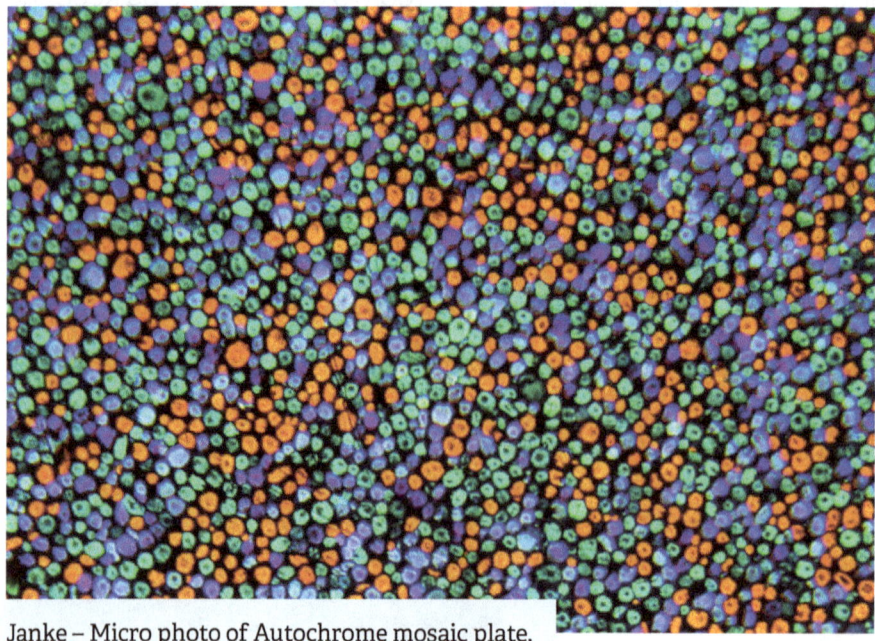

Janke – Micro photo of Autochrome mosaic plate.

Definition and History of Career

Taken in 1909. Young Russian peasant women in front of a traditional wooden house in a rural area along the Sheksna River near the small town of Kirkllov. Sergei Mikhailovich Prokudin-Gorskii created an early color photograph from Russia to document the Russian Empire from 1909 to 1915.

One of the drawbacks of the mosaic screen plate process was that it needed an exposure time of at least a second in bright daylight, more time if it was a cloudy day, and several minutes indoors. The color grains absorbed the color slowly, so the more brilliant the light, the faster it absorbed the dye. This picture could not be enlarged easily without making the many color dots (mosaic) obvious, making the image look "grainy."

Even after the invention of an inexpensive camera with film, cameras that used color plates were higher in quality and remained popular, even though they were more complicated.

The next era of photography came in 1935 with Kodachrome **35mm film**. This film captured pictures with three layers of emulsion – again, red, green, and blue. With additional processing, **complementary colors** like **cyan**, **magenta,** and yellow allowed for a **subtractive color image**, which meant more combinations of colors could come through on a picture because of the extra processing.

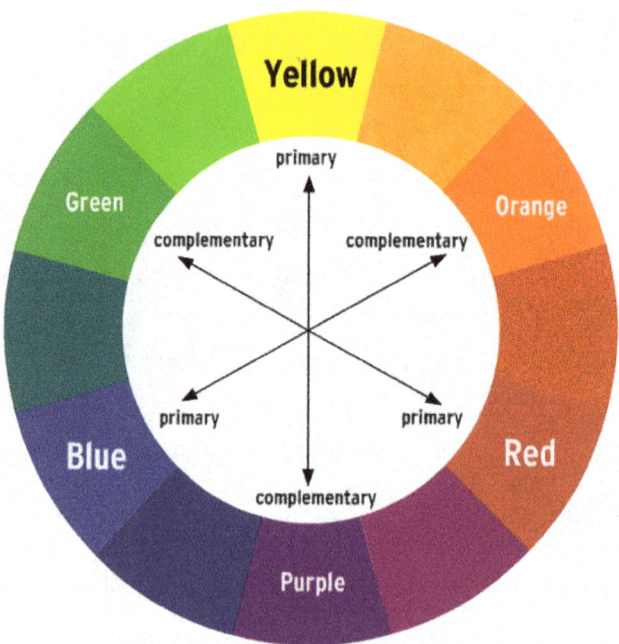

Lenses came next. Though they had been available for decades, cameras with single and twin (double) lenses were usually too bulky and did not become popular. A single-lens reflex (also called an SLR) is a camera with one lens that uses a mirror and a prism to "reflect" the image so the photographer can see the precise picture.

A twin-lens reflex (TLR) camera has two lenses. One lens takes the picture, and the other shows what the photographer sees when looking down into the camera.

Man looking down into a twin-lens reflex camera.

A historic camera: the Contax S of 1949 – the first pentaprism SLR

Polaroid came out with an instant camera in 1948. The Polaroid Model 95 was the first instant-picture camera and could, through a new chemical process, take a negative picture and complete a positive print – and print it! – in under a minute.

When computers arrived in 1957, Russell A. Kirsch at the National Institute of Standards and Technology explored creating digital images. The first pictures scanned into digital format showed pixels – tiny dots in a photo that make up the entire image.

CHAPTER ONE

The first digital cameras were created in 1969. Digital cameras do not use film but capture and save pictures on a **memory card** or internal storage device inside the camera. For photo processing, the memory card is plugged into a computer. Digital cameras were not sold widely until the 1990s. Through technological advances, cameras have evolved into the extremely clear, accurate, and colorful pictures we can take with our phones!

Chapter 1 Questions

1. Find some small items (paper clips, pens, erasers, etc.) to demonstrate Daguerre's silver-based photographic process. Do the same for the collodion wet plate process that came later. A simple sketch will work, too.

2. Write down two or three significant developments in photography in the last 150 years.

3. What color is complementary to red, and what colors are combined to make that color?

4. Write down three things you learned about photography in this chapter by reading about its history.

Photographer

Chapter 2
PURPOSE OF CAREER

> "The whole point of taking pictures is so that you don't have to explain things with words."
> —Elliott Erwitt

If we go back to the chapter about your purpose in life, remember that your purpose is what you want and why you want it. If you were looking at a photography career, you would ask yourself, "Why does a person take pictures, and what does he get paid for taking them?"

The purpose of a photographer is to capture an image that communicates a message creatively. That is a simple purpose. The exact message depends on who wants to say it and what they are willing to pay to say it.

Clients hire professional photographers to provide a picture for a client (customer) that communicates the message the client wants.

In turn, the client pays the photographer for providing that photo. For example, a photographer could work for an **advertising** agency to take pictures of products and sell them through advertising. A photographer could take photos of people for a business to put their employees on its website or **business cards**. Actors and real estate agents use professional photographs of themselves on business cards and websites to generate business.

What are some traits of a Photographer?

Photography is a skill that can be learned, just like any other skill. If you enjoy photography – even if you do not know much about it or do not think you are particularly good at it – it is something you can study to improve. Many personality traits, skills, and talents will make learning photography easier for some, but even if you do not feel like you have them, you can learn them. Your desire to learn something is all you need to begin any **endeavor** you wish to pursue.

Photographers typically desire to create an image that will cause a reaction in someone looking at it. Depending on the photographer's interests and skills and whether that image is newsworthy, artistic, beautiful, or informative, a person will usually gravitate to the most natural type of photography for them. For example, suppose a boy is really into sports, cars, and photography. In that case, it might be appealing for him to be a sports or race car photographer.

CHAPTER TWO

If a girl likes animals and photography, she might want to be an animal photographer, either a professional pet photographer or a creative photographer who enjoys taking **candid** and funny pictures of animals.

Ideally, your interests, skills, and talents come together in any career you choose.

A critical trait of a photographer is choosing the best picture for the job. If you capture 1000 photos of a subject for a client, you need to pick out the best ones – and know why you are picking them.

Any career you choose will require you to work with others, so you must learn to communicate well. You must know how to communicate to get your viewpoint and ideas across to others and listen and decipher what others say, so knowing how to sell will help. If you photograph people, you must know how to speak to them to get them to relax while you are taking their picture. If you work with babies or animals—the most challenging living things to photograph—you must find ways to communicate with them to get them to do what you want, like sitting still.

Remember that a positive and happy attitude will always take you far. Pointing out the good things, or what is right about something will be appreciated, especially when also communicating what you feel went wrong or needs correcting.

Photography is one career that leaves you alone responsible for delivering the product to your client. Suppose your client wants a picture of a baby playing with a puppy for an ad to promote their laundry detergent. In that case, you may be able to show up at the studio and start taking pictures without having to find the baby and the puppy, rent the studio, etc. However, when you are first getting started and need to build your portfolio, you will need to do it all – find the baby and the puppy and rent the studio. Also, because photography is such a competitive field, you will need lots of **tenacity**, persistence, and expert skill in capturing images. In other words, keep going and never give up!

As I mentioned, being a good communicator is critical to being a photographer. Even if you are not taking photos of people or animals, you must understand what your client is looking for and provide that so you get paid (and get hired again!). There are no excuses in photography—you either hand over what the client wants or you do not. If you do not, you probably will not get hired much.

You will need to be physically healthy as a photographer to walk, sit, crouch, bend – anything you need to get the shot. It would help if you were ready to stand or walk for long periods, sometimes carrying heavy equipment. When you use a digital camera, you will sit at a computer to sort through your pictures and make any changes to make them perfect. These changes can include cropping, color enhancement, or other special effects using computer software. We will discuss this in the training chapter.

Aside from being creative and detail-oriented enough to capture the perfect image, a photographer must communicate well and be comfortable working alone or with others. You may get into awkward positions to get the best shot or sit for long periods at a computer, but you have to do what it takes to get the job done.

There are many options for when and how you work in artistic careers, including photography. You can work for one company and go to work every Monday to Friday from 8 am to 5 pm, or you can freelance and work different hours. If you perform well at night, you can find projects where you take pictures during the day and edit at night.

How you get paid will also depend on how you like to work. You will likely get paid a salary if you work for one company, but working freelance means you get paid only for the jobs you do. If you work freelance, you will decide how you want your client to pay you. You could agree to get paid in full when you finish the job, or you might ask your client to pay you half the project fee **up-front** and the other half when you complete it.

Skills and Talents—These are only some talents that could be useful as a photographer. Your skills and talents will improve with a strong desire and practice.

- ☆ Creative
- ☆ Can turn an idea into a picture
- ☆ Likes to capture images that communicate a message
- ☆ Works well as part of a team
- ☆ Can sit, stand, or walk for long periods
- ☆ Likes working at a computer
- ☆ Inspires others with their pictures
- ☆ Communicates well
- ☆ Can work on deadline
- ☆ Ability to focus until the job is done
- ☆ Eye for creative expression that affects others
- ☆ Ability to execute innovative ideas
- ☆ Can easily convey feelings or emotions through an image
- ☆ Works well alone
- ☆ Engrossed with details
- ☆ Good at and enjoy solving problems
- ☆ Can take criticism easily
- ☆ Ability to tell a story through an image
- ☆ Can manage time wisely

Personality Traits – Some of these character traits could be useful when working as a photographer.

- ☆ Focused
- ☆ Self-motivated
- ☆ Self-Reliant and Self-Sufficient
- ☆ Independent
- ☆ Disciplined and Punctual
- ☆ Imaginative and Observant
- ☆ Ambitious
- ☆ Enjoy helping others create a message
- ☆ Enjoy working as part of a team
- ☆ Keen observer
- ☆ Communicates well
- ☆ Assertive
- ☆ Works well under pressure
- ☆ Enjoys capturing images
- ☆ Perfectionism in their work
- ☆ Calm and Cooperative
- ☆ Hardworking
- ☆ Enjoys variety in work
- ☆ Persistent
- ☆ Playful
- ☆ Gets along well with others
- ☆ Can easily handle criticism

> **Circle or highlight the skills, talents, and personality traits you think you possess.**

Photographers can accept an assignment and quickly determine the best way to deliver the product. I cannot say it enough: photographers must communicate well, exchange ideas quickly, and work tirelessly until the customer is happy. Depending on the job demands, they are okay working alone or with a group.

Remember that talents and skills can be improved with practice, and your personality traits can help you figure out the best career. Look at the purpose of this career again and ask yourself, "Would I be excited to work toward success as a photographer?" Above all, what you do every day should excite you, whether you are ten or sixty. You will not be in the mood every day to work, so you need to choose something you enjoy.

Essential Pieces and Tools of Photography

Photographers need various tools to get the job done. Aside from specialty equipment for certain types of photography, these are the primary tools one will need to start taking pictures professionally:

- Camera – a digital or film camera
- **Lenses** – more about this in a later chapter
- A **tripod**
- Computer software

- A computer monitor with color calibration for photography
- Lighting
- **Filters**
- Extras – including a camera bag (or backpack), lens cloths, extra batteries, and **memory cards**

Some job situations require special tools. For example, in sports photography, you will need a high-speed camera and many different lenses for the action you want to capture. The shutter speed needs to be 1/500th of a second or faster! This capture speed is why action sports pictures are so clear. Some photographers carry several cameras for a job requiring several shots. Spare lenses, spare batteries, and memory cards will always be items you will need to keep on hand.

Is Photography for You?

Based on what you learned above, does photography interest you? Why or why not?

Look again at what you created for your life purpose. You know yourself better than anyone else. What are you good at, and what comes easy to you? They might not be the same thing. What are your personality traits? Do some of these fit for a career as a photographer?

Remember, you will improve if you want to do something and work at it. So, having all the traits when starting is not needed! Just a desire to learn all about it and want to do it is a great starting point.

In the next chapter, you will learn more about how photographers work, where they work, how much money they make, and more.

Chapter 2 Questions

1. What is the purpose of a photographer?

2. On a computer search engine (Google or Microsoft Edge), type "photographs" in the search bar and select images. Pick out several pictures and see if you can imagine how the photographer took them.

3. What are some of the personality traits and talents of a photographer do you have?

4. What talents or skills as a photographer would you like to improve, and how can you do so?

Photographer

Chapter 3

CAREER BASICS

> " There are always two people in every picture. The photographer and the viewer. "
>
> —ANSEL ADAMS

What are the duties of a photographer?

A photographer's responsibilities depend on what their specialty is, but these are some of the most common duties of any photographer:

- Use various equipment, techniques, and lighting to take and edit photos.
- Use photo-enhancing software to produce photographs in different ways, such as printed or digital.
- Deliver the final product of the assignment to various people, including clients, graphic designers, corporate contacts, or the media (newspapers, magazines, TV, etc.).
- Provide retouching and any other adjustments to an image after photoshoots.

CHAPTER THREE

- Promote one's own business (if a freelancer) or the company one works for to get more clients.
- Buy or request the proper supplies for assignments.
- Market and advertise their services to get clients.
- Maintain a professional portfolio that advertises one's best photographic work.

If you want to make money taking photos, you are in luck! Over the last few years, with the rise of digital technology (and the cameras in our smartphones!), anyone can take pictures and sell them. Being a freelance photographer is the most lucrative way to make a career in photography. You could decide your specialty, learn all about it, become perfect by doing it continuously, and start your own photography business.

This book will give you a good start in learning all about photography. If you want to start your own business, you will need to learn how to run it successfully and know how to sell yourself and your business so you always have clients and assignments.

Career Basics

These are the most common photographer jobs for freelancers:

- Fashion photographer
- Sports photographer
- Product photographer
- Events photographer
- Assistant photographer
- **Stock photographer**

Some photographers still use traditional cameras that use film, but most use digital cameras, making it easy to see and edit on a computer using processing software for photography. A photographer may want to crop a picture, change it if needed, and do color correction, other enhancements, or special effects. Not only that, but digital images are also easy to store and send to others.

Camera **drones** can capture **aerial** shots.

Some other different types of photographers include:

- **Portrait** photographers
- **Photojournalists**
- **Commercial** and industrial photographers
- **Scientific** photographers
- Aerial photographers
- **Fine-Arts** photographers

I'm sure you can agree that there are many different avenues for pursuing a career in photography. You will have to ask yourself what you would like to do most. It might be working in a studio or visiting people's homes as a portrait photographer, taking artistic photos, taking important pictures in business (science or commercial), or fashion. You could specialize in taking stock, aerial, or crime scene photos. You could take pictures of pets or kids all day, rock stars, extreme sports, or simply food.

CHAPTER THREE

WHERE A PHOTOGRAPHER CAN WORK:
The largest employers of photographers are:

SELF-EMPLOYED WORKERS
68%

PHOTOGRAPHIC SERVICES
20%

BROADCASTING (TV, EXCLUDING THE INTERNET)
3%

NEWSPAPER, PERIODICAL, BOOK, AND DIRECTORY PUBLISHERS
1%

Most photographers work for themselves and run their businesses. Whether they hire others to help them or not, they are responsible for everything in their business:

- Advertising their photography services
- Finding potential clients and scheduling appointments
- Ensuring they have all the equipment needed for every assignment
- Purchasing supplies and maintaining and repairing equipment
- Billing clients, paying bills, and keeping records of everything

If photographers have other employees, they must hire, train, and pay them. They will also need to follow all the business rules, such as paying taxes, having insurance coverage, offering **human resources** to their employees, and more. Some photographers also like to teach classes or hold workshops in their studio or at a college or university.

Being responsible and a self-starter is essential if you are a self-employed photographer.

What hours does a photographer work?

As you can guess, you often do not have a set schedule when you are a photographer. This is good if you want complete control over your schedule. Depending on the assignment, you may need to stay up late to take pictures outside in the dark or early in the morning. If you have a specialty, like wedding photography, you will be remarkably busy in the summer and autumn months and not so busy in the winter. If you specialize in something that does not offer you a full-time schedule, you could have a few specialties to ensure you continually work or get a part-time job to make the money you want or need.

When you are friendly, easy to work with and provide fantastic pictures, clients will eventually find you because people will talk about how great you are. Word-of-mouth advertising is the best kind because it is free!

What hours you work will depend on your specialty. For example, wedding photographers want to work as many weekends in the summer as possible. If you have a portrait studio, you will often work there but also shoot on location if the assignment requires it. Suppose you are an industrial or product photographer. In that case, you will likely work more daytime hours, whereas if you are a forensic photographer or photojournalist, you might work any time of the day or night.

You will decide for yourself when and how you like to work. To be a photographer, you must adapt to many different locations, hours, and situations, even if you have a specialty. However, building your skills is easy because you can do it anytime. Take pictures of friends, family, pets, house, and neighborhood to find what you like.

How much money do photographers make?

According to the 2023 U.S. Bureau of Labor Statistics, the median (middle range, where half make more and half make less) annual wage for a photographer is $40,760. The top 10 percent earned more than $76,357, and the bottom 10 percent earned less than $19,843.

Cities/States with the highest average salaries are:

1. Washington D.C $88,540
2. New York $81,130
3. Vermont $77,780
4. California $75,510
5. Rhode Island $68,500

Top-paying industries for photographers:

1. Independent Artists and Performers $86,060
2. Software Publishers $84,970
3. Accounting, Bookkeeping and Payroll $84,800
4. Media Streaming and Social Networks $79,520
5. Managers for Entertainers & Public Figures $77,040

Industries with the highest levels of employment for photographers and their salaries:

1. Scientific and Technical Services $45,701
   (26,970 jobs, 3.5% of industry)
2. Media, Social Networks, Content Providers $79,520
   (2020 jobs, .86% of industry)
3. Radio and TV Broadcasting $60,600
   (1840 jobs, 1.51% of industry)
4. Newspaper and book publishers $53,870
   (1580 jobs, .54% of industry)

States that pay their photographers the least, according to zippia.com in 2024:

1. Oklahoma — $24,410
2. Iowa — $23,207
3. Florida — $22,984
4. Missouri — $22,485
5. Nevada — $20,532

I guess there is a lot of room for photographers to grow! The key to making it big as a photographer is having a specialty and becoming your best. Learn how to sell yourself, get hired for many jobs, and do an excellent job. Your clients will be happy to use you and refer you to others.

As you do this, your value as a photographer will increase. You will be in demand more, so you can charge more for your work. People are happy to pay a premium when you are the best at your job!

What life adjustments does a photographer need to make?

Adjustments for this career will depend significantly on the photographer's specialty. Those who work for one company usually have a regular schedule. Projects are typically due during the standard workday, Monday through Friday, 8 AM to 5 PM. Photographers who are freelance and work for themselves will work on the client's schedule and project deadline. Some jobs could affect family time, personal interests, or hobbies. Self-employed photographers must also find time to search for and book new projects.

What education does a photographer need?

Learning to be a photographer typically starts with classes about equipment, technology, and how to use it. Many photographers begin by working as a photographer's assistant. A formal education that results in a certificate or degree will give you an edge over other photographers who do not have formal training. It would be tough to learn the many technical things about photography without taking classes.

Photographers pursuing technical careers need more training and usually a college degree. The Professional Photographers of America offers a certification called Certified Professional Photographer. This certification might give you an edge over other photographers but is voluntary, so you do not need it.

If a photographer is self-employed, a college degree is optional. You will book jobs if you can expertly and efficiently use the equipment, software, and techniques needed to get the job done. If you use drones for assignments, you must meet the FAA (Federal Aviation Administration) requirements, including drone certification.

Becoming an assistant to a photographer can provide a wealth of experience and on-the-job training and allow you to build your portfolio with the help of a professional photographer.

A portfolio is a collection of your best photographic work. It might include pictures in a book, a website, or both.

You will learn much more information about education in the next chapter.

Example of an online portfolio.

What is the job outlook for photographers?

Due to quality cameras installed in just about every smartphone and the ability to purchase stock photos from sites such as Adobe Stock Photos and Shutterstock, the photography field is expected to grow by 4% by 2032, which is average for most careers. According to www.opticsmag.com, U.S. jobs in photography are expected to increase by 17% in the coming years. Portrait photography is one specialty that will likely continue to grow despite a decline in other areas of photography. Families, schools, and businesses will still want photos.

Photographers going into business for themselves find niches to work in and become experts. But, again, going into business for yourself may mean doing everything yourself, including locating your clients and selling them on your services, invoicing and collecting payments, ordering and maintaining equipment, and hiring and managing your employees.

Chapter 3 Questions

1. Name some different careers one could do as a photographer and what type of person would do that career (personality, skills, talents).

2. Name some photography careers for which you might need a college degree and some you would not. Why do you think so?

3. Look online to see if you can find some photography courses near you. Are there online classes? Where are they? How much do they cost, and what will you learn?

4. Create an assignment for yourself. Decide what the product will be (a picture of a meal for a magazine article, for example) and choose a deadline. Do the assignment.

Photographer

Chapter 4

Some Career Possibilities

> "A good photograph is one that communicates a fact, touches the heart, and leaves the viewer a changed person for having seen it. It is, in a word, effective."
>
> —Irving Penn

Now, let's break it down and look at several careers in more detail. The following are the most in-demand and highest-paying jobs in photography.

Photojournalist

A photojournalist is a photographer who captures the news. These guys and gals often work for newspapers or magazines; their photographs tell stories about current events.

Breaking into photojournalism can be challenging because many photographers are interested in it, but if you want it, you can find a way to get there. You will have to pay your dues and possibly start as a freelancer or intern, but if you are interested in bringing the news to people through pictures, there are many parts of photojournalism you could pursue. You could cover local events in your town or city, such as regional sports events, specialize in other news or events, or even travel internationally.

Since this career is highly competitive, you must think creatively to capture a shot better than other photographers. You also need to care about the news and be ok with all types of stories – good and bad. Typically, you will need to travel, even if it is just around the city you live in, and you will need to be flexible about when you work because news can happen any time, day or night.

Sports Photographer

This specialty is easy to figure out. A sports photographer is someone who takes pictures of athletes and sporting events. They can work for newspapers, magazines, sports websites, or **stock photo agencies**. Sports photography can fall under photojournalism or commercial photography, depending on the communication.

Sports photographers usually have the best spots at professional sports games and sit amongst other sports photographers right in front of the action. Because the action happens so fast, special lenses and other equipment are needed to capture a great shot at a distance. If you have ever been to a professional sporting event, you have likely seen remote cameras placed where the photographer is not, such as at the goalpost or above the basketball net.

The great thing about learning sports photography is that there are plenty of sporting events to improve your skills! From Little League to high school and college sports, it should be easy to find games and athletes to photograph.

Studio/Portrait Photographer

Portrait photographers take pictures of people, usually in a way that makes them look as good as possible. Think of your school and sports pictures. A portrait photographer takes those. However, there are many other specialty fields. You could be a fashion photographer and take photos of the latest fashions, fashion shows, or fashion models. Celebrity photographers are precisely that – they take pictures of celebrities for magazines or news stations, or stars can hire them directly.

Sports Photography

Wedding photographers specialize in love and happiness. Wedding photographers sometimes extend their specialty to family portrait photos, baby photos, engagement photos, and graduation photos. You get the picture. **Pun** intended. Get it? Ha-ha.

A corporate photographer can work for one company or organization or have many clients as a freelancer. A corporate photographer takes pictures of employees. Though many businesses don't hire professional photographers to take photos of employees, some industries, such as real estate, advertising, and media, are known for their professional images. Some companies want professional photographs of their employees for the company website.

Commercial Photographer

Commercial photography is the branch of photography that uses pictures to sell products or services. Commercial means "relating to commerce," and commerce is the interchange of goods in business. Think "trading": buying and selling.

There are a few different types of commercial photography. In advertising, you see pictures in magazines, billboards, websites, etc., to sell a product or service. You could take photos for catalogs, such as people wearing the clothes or the products themselves, and product packaging pictures will show a picture of a product. All types of commercial photography aim to get people to buy the things in the pictures or take the desired action, such as visiting a particular restaurant or buying tickets to an event.

As a commercial photographer, you can take pictures of people or things. If you worked for an advertising agency that just hired Justin Bieber to sell the toothpaste of their newest client, you could find yourself in the studio taking pictures of Justin Bieber brushing his teeth!

Food photographers would fall under commercial photography if a cookbook publisher hired them to take the food pictures for their latest cookbook.

Some Career Possibilities

Portrait Photography

Commercial Photography

CHAPTER FOUR

Forensic Photographer

A Forensic photographer takes pictures at crime scenes, and these pictures can be **evidence** in a court case.

Along with basic photography skills, a forensic photographer must be unbelievably detailed in taking pictures and be interested in helping solve crimes. The images you take need to give the exact information of a crime scene without leaving out any possible details. Your photos can help point out the timeline of events or where the fingerprints might be.

You would take photography classes at a police academy or a school that trains forensic photographers. You would often need to study or have experience in forensic science, law enforcement, and criminology.

The hours of this job vary depending on the number of cases. Forensic photographers work for a police department or **coroner's** office. A photographer can work part-time for different law enforcement departments. As an **entry-level** forensic photographer, you likely will

Forensic Photography

not earn much money: on average, about $20,000/year, but as a more experienced photographer with full-time work, you can make an average of about $50,000/year.

Fine Art Photographer

Artists and photographers come together in the field of fine art photography. Think of a painting or something artistic, and then imagine that as a photograph. That is what a fine art photographer does – they create a picture that is considered a work of art. Though there can be some overlap with photojournalism or fashion photography, the purpose of this field is not to communicate the news and not to provide facts or advertise products. Fine art photography focuses on bringing forth a specific emotion in the viewer or expressing a message or idea.

Photographers have expressed their artistic side in their pictures since the beginning of photography. However, photography wasn't considered creative until the 1960s. Before, it was considered a craft, not the **aesthetic** form of communication we think of today.

Fine Art Photography

Stock Photographer

As stock photography has become more popular, demand for specialty photographers has decreased. Stock photography agencies put many photos in one place and categorize them by subject. People who need a specific type of photo can go to a website like Adobe Stock Photos or Shutterfly, find one picture they can use, and buy it. They do not need to hire someone for just one shot. Most of the images in this *Your Best Rockin' Life* book are stock photographs. You could be a photographer who takes pictures that many people can purchase for many reasons. Stock photography could be a good niche if you are good at taking many different types of pictures.

If you want to be a stock photographer, consider researching the most popular stock photos purchased. If you find this out, you will see trends in what people buy, and if you supply pictures that fit into those categories, you should always have people buying your work.

Videographer

Someone who takes moving pictures is called a videographer. Taking a video would include capturing moving images and the surrounding sounds. There are many positions for those interested in moving pictures in the entertainment industry. **Camera Operator**, **Lighting Specialist,** or **Film Editor** might be options related to videography. A videographer can work alone (as a freelance photographer) or as part of a larger group of people on a film set.

Cinematographers are different from videographers in terms of their equipment, primarily **mechanical film cameras** (cameras that use film). Most videographers use digital cameras or those with **flash drive video**.

The Best Paying Specialties for Photographers

According to a blog post at photoworkout.com dated June 4, 2024, the following careers in photography pay the most, in order of the highest paying:

1. **Commercial Photographers** take pictures of products for marketing and advertising purposes.
2. **Fashion Photographers** work with clients like clothing brands, fashion shows, and boutiques.
3. **Wedding Photographers** attend bridal shows and can find clients by being active at church.
4. **Portrait Photographer** who can work for individuals, magazines, or companies.
5. **Photojournalists** capture world events, sometimes as they are happening.
6. **Film Set Photography** is a behind-the-scenes look at the art of filmmaking. Search the government websites in your state to find current film productions.
7. **Architecture Photographers** typically take real estate pictures and work with real estate agents, architects, contractors, and hotels.

As you can see, there are many ways you can take your interests and create the exact perfect photography career for you.

Fashion Photography

CHAPTER FOUR

Chapter 4 Questions

1. Name a few different types of Portrait Photographers.

2. In Commercial Photography, how are the pictures used? Give some examples.

Some Career Possibilities

3. What does this photograph communicate to you, and who might be moved by its communication?

4. After reading about some specialties you could pursue as a Photographer, which one or two sounds the most exciting to you? Why? Can you think of ways to specialize in one or more of these?

5. BONUS Question: Why do you think Fashion Photographers make the most money?

Your Best Rockin' Life

Photographer

Chapter 5

Training and Getting a Job

> "Photography for me is not looking; it's feeling. If you can't feel what you're looking at, then you're never going to get others to feel anything when they look at your pictures.."
>
> —Don McCullin

Becoming a photographer can be done in several different ways. One can take online courses, get a technical associate degree, get a bachelor's or master's degree, or not any degree, but learn independently or with "on the job" training.

It depends on what you want to do as a photographer. Suppose you're going to work for a magazine like National Geographic. In that case, your training will be different than if you want to convert your garage into a studio and take family photos in your hometown. Decide what kind of photographer you want to be by looking at what you like to capture on film or what you're good at. Then, decide where you want to work and how much money you want to make. That will help determine the training you should pursue.

If you want to be a famous photographer and make millions of dollars, you must know the steps to take to get you there. Whatever you want is ok if it is what you want to do. We have already discussed many careers and specialties you could pursue as a photographer.

Different from many careers, a degree in photography is optional for a photography career, especially if you are planning on freelancing (being self-employed). Many community colleges, four-year colleges, and universities offer **undergraduate degrees** and **graduate school** programs in photography. You can also find short courses, seminars, or workshops to take one at a time. Focus on specific subjects in photography, like using a digital camera, shooting in black and white, or using photo editing software.

No matter what you decide and no matter how much schooling you get, the first choice is what your specific focus will be. What kind of pictures do you want to take? What do you enjoy – people, landscapes, or products? Houses, sports, or events? Once you have that nailed down, you will need to know about all the equipment you'll need, how to use it, and what software and computer programs you will need to use to edit or share your pictures.

You will also need good communication skills to communicate ideas and suggestions to your client and those you take pictures of – and in some cases, that will be the same person.

DIY Photography Education

Knowing your path as a photographer is essential in figuring out what training you need. Many freelance photographers do not need a formal education if they can get trained and build their portfolios. But all training will be helpful, no matter your path. You will need to cover these basics as a freelancer:

- **Equipment** – you will need to know what equipment you need, how and when to use it, and what to do if it breaks.

- **Software**—you will need the exact software required for your editing. You must also understand how every aspect of the software works so you get the perfect picture every time.
- **Salesmanship** – whether you have a business or work for someone else, you will still need to know how to communicate effectively and sell yourself and your work. It would be best to convince your clients that you will get them the exact picture they are looking for and that you are the perfect person for their assignment. Convincing them that you are the right person will come out in your communication and personality. Are you easy to talk to, friendly, and sincere, yet will you persevere until you get what they want? You will want to build up your portfolio and references list to become known in your industry.
- **Practice, Practice, Practice**—keep at it. Professional athletes practice continuously, both during and off-season. Before getting paid to be a photographer, you must still be a photographer. Create your own assignments and build the exact portfolio to get the paying photo work you want.

The great news is that there are online photography courses and inexpensive courses at community colleges (and even in high school!) you could do now. You might also offer to intern with a professional photographer and get on-the-job training – the best kind of training there is!

Online Courses

Taking an online photography course can provide an inexpensive way to learn some basics about photography, like **Fundamentals, Imaging, Digital Processing, Digital Design,** and the **Business of Photography**.

CHAPTER FIVE

Some online classes are hybrids that require minimal in-person meetings. You can still learn some excellent skills. You will need your equipment, possibly software, and a computer with a good internet connection.

Plan to learn basic skills in color, black and white, and digital photography. Also, prepare to learn about editing software and photo editing.

With your course schedule, you will be on your own to figure out when to do your work (great practice in self-motivation!) to turn it in by the due date.

If you pass your online training, you will receive a certificate and can earn an associate's degree if the online school offers it. Some schools even provide dual concentration certificate programs that offer additional studies related to photography, such as illustration, graphic design, or web design.

Associate degree or Vocational Training

An associate degree in photography takes about two years to complete. Some associate degree programs offer online classes, and others combine online and in-person courses. Some schools use conferencing software like Zoom or Google Meet to allow interaction in class.

Class subjects for an associate degree include learning and improving digital design skills alongside the basics of photography. You will also likely take classes in communications, web design, marketing, and other industry-related subjects.

You can purchase many online books, course materials, photography equipment, and software. Some classes even request you have a particular type of computer operating system (MAC or Windows) and updated versions of **internet browsers**, such as Internet Explorer Safari, Microsoft Edge, Google, or Mozilla Firefox.

Vocational or trade school training is only for a specific job. For example, if you wanted to be a plumber, you would take classes only related to plumbing and nothing else. You would not take courses in marketing, sales, or geometry. You would only take vocational training for the job of being a plumber. For a photographer, this would mean just the basics or specific training related to one type of photography, like underwater photography. Vocational training is excellent because you can quickly acquire knowledge and training to start working.

Bachelor's Degrees

Taking college courses in photography is always a great way to learn technical skills. Many schools put photography classes in the art department, and depending on the program you take, you could earn a Bachelor of Fine Arts (BFA), a Bachelor of Arts (B.A.), or a Bachelor of Science (B.S.). Some programs, such as Bachelor of Fine Arts, could require submitting a portfolio as part of your application into the fine arts program. So, you may need to show your experience and have a camera.

You can expect to learn how to take pictures using both a **manual camera** and a digital camera, in both color and black and white. You will also learn how to print those pictures. The school will typically have labs where you can develop photos and use digital software to edit.

You can expect to take these courses on campus:

- Art history
- Color photography
- **Composition**
- Digital editing
- Marketing

Other photography courses include color photography, processing/developing photos, and specialty classes about wildlife, advertising, and more.

You will also take many classes of your choosing. You could take design classes, drawing, modeling, painting, and art **theory**. Business courses teach professionalism and how to start and run your own business.

Master's Degree

After you get a bachelor's degree in photography, you may want to get a master's degree. An advanced degree in photography takes about one to two years to complete and allows you to understand and use the most advanced tools. You will learn about many more specialties like travel, industry, portraiture, nature, underwater photography, and food photography. You can do an online program, though you may need to go on campus for specific projects.

Some of the courses you could take include:

- High-speed photography
- Properties of light
- Color management (how to use colors for the best effect)
- Web design
- Documentary-style photography

A master's degree could help you get better job opportunities, especially since the expectation is for fewer jobs for photographers in the next 5-10 years. Because digital equipment tends to be inexpensive, many amateur photographers can take photos as well as professional photographers.

A photographer meeting with a client.

How to Pay for Your Education

Now that you know what kind of education you can get, you must find a way to pay for it. Buying books to study and taking free or low-cost online classes is a great way to start, but you will also want to plan for advanced training or college costs. Here are some general costs of an education in photography:

- Online Training, Books, Seminars – Free, $20-$50 for books, up to $500+ for seminars
- Online Classes – Varies, usually $250-$500/class
- Vocational or Online Degree Programs – Varies, anywhere from $3,500-$10,000+
- Community or Junior Colleges – About $3,500 per year
- Undergraduate Degree (Bachelor's) – About $10,000 per year
- Graduate Degree (Master's) – About $8,500 for the degree, no matter how long it takes

Many programs can be purchased one semester (half a school year) at a time. There is other help, too. You could apply for financial aid through a **student loan**, **grant**, or **scholarship**.

But... Do You Need a Degree to be a Photographer?

Getting a degree is required by many companies, and it shows you are committed to your desire to be a photographer. However, you may not need a degree since photography is a highly creative job. Once you know what you want to specialize in, you can decide what training will be best for you.

You will get work as a photographer by having a portfolio that shows your work truthfully and authentically and finding a company or client that wants to work with you because they like your work. Will they ask to see your degree? Maybe, but that would depend on the job they have for you. You could be a real estate photographer and do such a great job that real estate agents talk about you to others, and you get assignments from those **referrals**.

For some people, college is not appealing or attractive, but that does not mean they are afraid to study or don't see the benefits of college. Some people, truthfully, are just not "college people."

However, being self-educated could hold you back from work if you seek employment with companies requiring certain classes or developed photography skills. Educating yourself means focusing on what you know or are the best at, but you might miss out on opportunities for which others are better trained. Think about the future and what you want. Consider all the jobs you would like to do. You will have more jobs and opportunities (and money!) with more skills.

Remember, photography is an art form. It is communicating a message through pictures. Classes and degrees will teach you basics and skills, but finding your style will be crucial for success. Follow your heart and see what is best for YOU.

Look again at the different ways you can **learn your trade**, then choose the path you feel would fit the best for your future. Focus on schools and curriculums that offer classes in the areas you want to work. Look at your talents, interests, personality, and life purpose, and create a plan that excites you.

Your training and experience determine your ability to handle work requirements and responsibilities. You will not always like what you do, even if you love it. There will be parts of your job that you genuinely enjoy, but there will always be tasks or other activities you need to do that you do not like. And there will be days you are not in the mood for it. Like it or not, that is how it goes with everyone and every job. Finding a job that fits you and aligns with your life purpose is the point.

If you do not have professional working experience, your training and portfolio will be a significant factor in what kinds of jobs you can get and what you will be paid. You may not want to be a photographer's assistant, but you must understand how to work your way up to your ideal job. Take every opportunity to learn more about photography, equipment, and working with other photographers. Communicate with people you meet about what you are trying to do so they think of you when something comes up.

Once you have decided on your direction for your photography career, act immediately to make it happen. Sign up for an online course, buy a book, or find a camera store or photography studio that might be hiring. As you learn, you will feel something is going in a good direction for you or it is not. If not, find another path that makes more sense for you.

It will be best to create your resume when you have some skills and pictures for a portfolio. Your resume and portfolio will be the tools to set you apart from others who are also looking to break into photography.

Networking

Networking is essential no matter what career you choose. Whether you are in a creative career, like photography or a corporate job, talking to others can always help. Networking is talking to others to find people who could hire you. Once you decide what you want to do and where you will get your training, you need to take the step and talk about it to anyone who will listen.

Networking is making friends in this one area – photography. You will want to find places to connect with people who can help and guide you, introduce you to others, and whom you can help. The best part about networking is that if you network with the right people, these people can help you find the job you want and even give you a **referral**. Finding your desired positions can be easier if

A networking event.

you have other people helping you. Networking is just talking to people, being friends, and sharing ideas about how you can help each other. You can network using social media, but in-person networking is the best.

You may not know who to talk to when you attend a networking event, especially at first. That does not matter. Just find someone that looks friendly and say hi. You do not always have to talk about photography or careers. Get to know people and decide if you like them or have some things in common. Then, see who they know. If they know others, ask them to introduce you to someone else. If not, move on to the next person. Networking events are for relaxing and talking to as many people as possible. It is not a contest, and no one is keeping score. Set a goal for meeting one or two new people each time, and then be proud of yourself when you do!

Networking should be easy and fun. Some people do not like networking events, but one way to think about it is that you are meeting people who could help you get a job. Take basic communication classes to help you feel comfortable talking to anyone easily and confidently. You want to show others who you are and what you want in life. Read some basic sales books or take introductory sales courses to help you understand how to use your communication skills to get what you want. You will need this when interviewing for a job, so keep practicing!

The Interview

Once you complete your portfolio and resume, you are ready to look for a job. If you have been networking, you may know some available jobs or where to start looking. Consider if your friends may know someone you would like to meet. Building up a networking community is essential for any career.

Training and Getting a Job

How do you find jobs? Start with people you know. Ask around. Get on social media. Find groups of people that meet about similar interests. Find successful photographers doing what you want to do. If you can, ask a photographer to mentor you. If you don't have anyone to ask, you can still look at what they are doing and try to do that. You can use what made someone successful by finding your version of what they are doing.

Once you secure an interview for a job or project, be prepared. Learn a bit about the company and how they work. See if you can talk to one or two people who know something about the client or what they want. Be professional, but be yourself. You want them to hire you, so treat it as something important. Wear the nicest business clothes you have. You do not have to get fancy, but make sure you are clean and your hair is combed. You have done all the right things to get to this point. Congratulations! Now, be yourself and let the rest take care of itself. Do not try to say something to impress the person you are talking to. Just say what comes naturally. Be friendly, honest, and sincere. If it does not work out, learn from it and use what you have learned in your next interview.

CHAPTER FIVE

Chapter 5 Questions

1. Name the different ways you can get training to be a photographer.

2. Using your sketchpad, create a simple drawing that shows the difference between a graduate degree and an undergraduate degree in photography.

3. Describe why networking is essential and list some ways to start networking now. Who will you talk to, where, and about what?

4. Based on what you have learned in this chapter, what direction do you want to go for your education? What are some ideas for paying for it?

5. What job do you think you would like to start working as a photographer? What job would you like to be doing in five or ten years?

Fashion Photography by Tim Sabatino

TimSabatino.com

Photographer

Chapter 6

Meet Some Professionals

I found three very different and diverse photographers to interview for this chapter. You will get a sneak peek at what they have learned about breaking into a career as a photographer, what they knew and didn't know, like and dislike, and what tips they have for you. Each photographer is on their unique path. However, each has created an outstanding career and has achieved great success.

And now, our first professional photographer.

Photography by Tim Sabatino

CHAPTER SIX

Tim Sabatino
Cinematographer/Director/Producer/Photographer at Fast Flow Productions and Infiniti Ranch & Artist at Tim Sabatino Fine Art

TIM SABATINO is a California native and a US Navy Veteran of the Gulf War. Photography is his main occupation and has been for over 25 years. He specializes in advertising, fashion, beauty, and celebrity photography. Tim is also a director and producer of music videos, commercials, films, and commercial advertising. He has won Best Photography in the Valley awards (Los Angeles) several times.

The number of hats Tim has worn in the entertainment industry is mind-boggling. Since 1989, he has worked as a Producer, Director, Cameraman, and Director of Photography. Still, he has also experienced success in acting, modeling, stunt driving, and doing lighting, grip, and electric behind the scenes. He most recently worked as an actor in the feature film *Watchful Eye* and was a stunt driver in *Fast and Furious 7* and *Batman Dark Knight Rises*.

Tim has had exhibitions of his oil paintings and photography at many galleries worldwide and won his first art contest at five years old.

Tim grew up as an artist and portrait painter. When he was sixteen, he took his first photography class and learned basic black and white photography using a dark room with the initial interest in capturing subjects he could then paint.

After high school, he joined the Navy and planned to go to college on the **GI Bill**. At the time, he was interested in architecture and fine art. Photography became a hobby, and he got a job at a camera store to help with college costs. He worked there for seven years and developed a great love and appreciation for the visual medium.

Over those seven years, Tim took advantage of a great perk of working at a camera store: he could take home and use any equipment from the store on the weekends. This gave him a hands-on learning experience for free! He could also buy equipment, lighting, tripods, lenses, and cameras with his employee discount. A bonus was meeting and working with famous photographers and store customers such as Greg Gorman, Jim Marshall, Annie Liebowitz, Steven Meisel, and others.

He learned that photographers find a specialty at which to become experts. Specialties could include fashion, beauty, food, editorial, fine art, portrait, products, or real estate photography.

For Tim, that specialty was fashion and celebrities, including actor **headshots**. At thirty years old, he became a full-time self-employed photographer. He was responsible for everything: marketing and

CHAPTER SIX

advertising his photography services, finding and selling new clients, scouting locations, casting, post-production, editing and retouching, and billing. Tim has found that utilizing social media is a must. He posts much of his work on Facebook, LinkedIn, and YouTube and does paid advertising.

Photography by Tim Sabatino

Tim's mom unexpectedly influenced his eventual career in fashion photography. He grew up watching her as a hairstylist. He chatted with her clientele and read and studied pictures in the salon's fashion magazines. Los Angeles was a natural place for Tim because it provided the clientele, fashion, and actors he loved to photograph.

As far as training is concerned, Tim says it is vital. As with other creative and technical fields, technology constantly changes, making it hard to keep up without formal training. Although most photographers are independent (self-employed), keeping up with education and how things are changing in the industry is vital.

- What Tim has learned from his photography career:
    - Specialties and expertise can lead to different jobs,

so get involved in different parts of the industry. If you learn to produce, scout locations, or cast shoots, you can open the doors to other creative work in the same field.

- Tim's advice for anyone interested in pursuing a photography career:
    - If you are new to photography, work at a camera store, and always set aside a portion of your income for equipment.
    - Know that your portfolio is your resume, so consider how to build it. Take free jobs and continually find ways to improve the quality of your pictures. Always strive to improve your work.
    - Understand that because photographers are artists, they can get attacked. Creative personalities often have this problem. Keep working, never stop, and never give up. Find a way to rise above to flourish and prosper in your work.
    - Find what you want to specialize in and keep practicing until you are the best.
    - If you want to shoot portraits or headshots, try to get to celebrities because those pictures will be a great way to advertise your work.

Tim has photographed celebrities, fashion models, musicians, dancers, and even The Dalai Lama. He has genuinely achieved outstanding success in photography and his other endeavors. He is a humanitarian and volunteer and regularly contributes to several human rights charities. Tim is a proud husband to his wife, April, and father to three beautiful children: Violette, Faye, and Atlas. Find him on social media, visit his website at www.timsabatino.com, and find him on YouTube at @Timsabatino.

Thank you, Tim!

CHAPTER SIX

Jordan Wise
Owner, Jordan Wise & Co.

Meet Some Professionals

As featured in Forbes, CNN, Food & Wine, World's 50 Best, New York Times, Washington Post, San Francisco Chronicle, San Francisco Weekly, and more, we are thrilled to spotlight **JORDAN WISE**. She is a remarkably busy lady, running her Creative Marketing and Photography business in Florida's Tampa Bay metropolitan area.

Jordan grew up in Raleigh, North Carolina. She was in high school when she developed an interest in photography and took classes in film photography. Though Jordan had access to digital cameras, she also learned how to operate a film camera, plus all the elements of developing pictures on photo paper in a dark room. She took a New York Institute of Photography correspondence course and, wondering if she wanted to be a chef or a photographer, also went to culinary school. Her niche, naturally, became culinary photography.

Specializing in restaurant and hotel photography, Jordan travels nationwide for her shoots. Her **high-profile** clients include Airbnb, American Express, Delta, Penguin Random House, Resy, Relais et Chateaux, Crenn Dining Group, Ducasse Hospitalite, Michael Mina, and many other hotels and restaurants.

Photography by Jordan Wise

CHAPTER SIX

Photography by Jordan Wise

In her daily work life, Jordan spends most of her time editing or post-processing, which is the work done after a photo shoot to select the best pictures (called "**selects**"). She will then edit each select individually to adjust the exposure, contrast, and colors to fit the client's expectations.

After editing and post-processing, the shoot takes up much of Jordan's time. As her clients are all over the country, she must drive or fly to the location, ensure she has all the right equipment and everything organized, and then set up and do the shoot.

Marketing and client **procurement** are other big focuses for Jordan, and her goal is to continue adding to her client base so that her business is continually recognized.

Jordan was surprised to learn how much administrative work photographers need to do, not only in the detailed photo editing process but also in running a business and invoicing her clients.

She also mentioned the amount of competition in the field of photography. Losing a job to someone with little photography experience can be frustrating. Nowadays, anyone can get a small digital camera or smartphone and call themselves a photographer.

The competition aspect would not have stopped Jordan from getting into photography, but she has found she does need to find creative ways to beat out her competition to book quality, well-paying jobs. She is continually striving to build solid relationships with her clients. She wants them to know they will get nothing less than superb, high-quality photos when they hire her.

- Here are a few tips from Jordan for anyone interested in diving into a career in photography:
    - Study is essential, but practice is more important. One can hire a photographer for their **creative eye** and ability to capture a story in a single picture, even when they don't have full knowledge of the subject.
    - Find your voice and find a niche. You will learn what you are good at and what you like when you practice. It might be weddings, sports, fashion, portraits, or something else. Once you find your specialty, focus on being your best in that area and expand to other related areas.
    - You will know you have found your niche when you LOVE the pictures yourself, are proud of them, and are confident they tell the stories you want to tell.
    - Marketing is essential. You must always tell people about yourself and your work to build your contact list and get more referrals.
    - Keep persisting if photography is something you want to do. There will be difficult times, but find a way to make things happen. Never give up on yourself and your dreams!

Thank you, Jordan, for inspiring us with your success! As Jordan focuses on her growing family, we wish her tremendous success with her creative culinary photography and marketing business. Check out Jordan on her website at Tampa Digital Marketing Agency (jordanwise.co) and other social media.

CHAPTER SIX

Matt Cali
Owner, Matt Cali Photography

MATT CALI was only eighteen when he got his first paid job as a photographer. It was a wedding, and even feeling "terrified," he was pleasantly surprised the photos turned out as well as they did. The above image is an excellent example of a technically imperfect photo that still resonates. Why? This pic was snapped "in the moment" by someone nearby with a camera. The lighting is not perfect because it's not staged, but the emotion (happiness) is captured.

Just one year before his first paid shoot, Matt received his first camera as a gift from his father, a 35-millimeter Pentax k1000 film camera. Growing up in Seattle, Washington, Matt spent every spare moment that year shooting on the city's wet and rainy streets. After taking a photography class in high school, it didn't take long for him to realize photography was what he wanted to do with his life.

Photography by Matt Cali

CHAPTER SIX

I sat down with Matt, and he gave me insight into the different paths and possibilities of a career as a photographer and how he turned his passion for taking pictures into a rewarding and successful career.

A Pentax k1000 is a camera that shoots on film that needs to be developed, which means you can't see the pictures until you develop them in a darkroom. This is very different from the technology we have today, where you can take a photo using a digital camera or with your phone and instantly see it.

Matt earned a bachelor's degree in Fine Arts, with a focus on Photography from Central Washington University, but says the bulk of education has been just doing the work and learning along the way. Some photographers hire others to help them with staging a shoot or setting up the lights, but Matt loves doing all the work himself. He enjoys his time with his clients and says one key to his success is learning from the client "who they want to be" and helping them create that person for the camera.

Some of Matt's main focuses are portraits, headshots, and fashion photography, but he also enjoys shooting specialty photography, weddings, commercials (advertising), and travel. Invited to showcase his work, Matt gave five solo **exhibitions** in Seattle before leaving for Tinseltown, also known as Los Angeles.

Matt photographed actors and models for the first five years of his career in Los Angeles to build his portfolio. Now, he goes worldwide if he likes the assignment but mainly shoots in Los Angeles, Las Vegas, and Seattle.

Like many photographers, Matt worked **side jobs** while building his experience and portfolio as a photographer. He chose to do work that kept him close to his love of pictures and worked in a photo lab to learn and gain experience.

Matt immersed himself in his life as a photographer and continues to train and learn from other successful photographers. He still takes classes and pays attention to what other professionals are doing so he can improve his work.

Promotion and marketing are big focuses for Matt, and he uses Instagram and other social media to promote his work. He understands that getting your work out creates attention for your photography style and **brand**. The more people see your pictures and name, the more attention you will get. When you get a lot of attention, you'll get more work.

Matt keeps in touch with his clients by phone and email and sends newsletters to showcase his latest projects. Aside from promotion, Matt's work time is spent preparing for shoots, shooting, and editing the pictures.

Photography by Matt Cali

- What has Matt learned from his career as a photographer?
    - Even if you love what you do, it's still work, and sometimes it's much more work than you think it will be. Matt has been surprised at how difficult it is sometimes to juggle everything as a freelance photographer.
    - Depending on where you are in your life and career, you may need to make compromises. You may be asked to shoot a wedding when you are not a wedding photographer. You may decide to take a job for the money or to build your portfolio. You need to decide for yourself if these compromises are worth it.

Matt has advice for anyone interested in pursuing a photography career:

- It takes time to build your career, so stay focused. Decide what kind of photos you want to take and spend your time doing that. Trying new things for an assignment can be a good learning experience, but make sure you keep progressing on your focus area. If you want to work in fashion, then work in fashion and don't get side-tracked into something else unless it's a good learning experience and will help further your career.
- Focus on what you want your future to look like and create actions that will lead you to that.
- Stay true to yourself and your beliefs. Shooting something you don't believe in just for a paycheck doesn't make sense, so try to steer clear of those situations.
- Collaborate with others to do free shoots (called "colab" shoots) to build your client base and portfolio. Even when you start getting paid, it might make sense to do a free or discounted shoot for the experience or exposure (shooting a celebrity, for example).
- Free work rarely leads to paid work. The most challenging clients are often the same ones asking for discounted

rates. Believe in yourself and your value, and do your best to stick to the rates you've decided on.

- You must showcase your work as much as possible to get attention. Do this any way you can – social media, email, videos – whatever fits you best. The more attention you get, the more people will think of you when they need a photographer.
- As your work gets better, increase your rates. The more valuable you are, the more you can charge.
- Trust your gut and be confident in your work. When you believe in it, others will, too.

Matt has photographed dozens of celebrities and household names, including A-list actors, professional athletes, radio personalities, and musicians. He's worked in New York City, London, Bora Bora, Haiti, Bangkok, and Nicaragua, to name a few. Find his work or contact him on Instagram @mattcali_photography or his website: www.mattcaliphotography.com.

Thank you very much, Matt!

Photography by Matt Cali

Chapter 6 Questions

1. Name a few things you were surprised to learn about a photography career.

2. Do you feel you understand photography better? Are you more interested in pursuing it or less interested? Why?

3. Name a couple of personality traits and skills you feel would make a photographer successful. Name a few talents you have and could develop for this career.

4. Write down three things you feel you are good at (they don't have to be related to photography).

YOUR BEST ROCKIN' LIFE

Your Best Rockin' Life

IN CLOSING

> **Self-belief and hard work will always earn you success.**
> —Virat Kohli

I hope this book has been a fun journey for you. Did you learn anything new about yourself?

Now it's time to step up to the starting line and start your career path!

Life is a beautiful journey that you will embark upon alone at times. When you're a kid, you count on your parents and others to help you, give you a place to sleep, ensure you have food, and get an education. As you grow older, you will have more responsibility for your life and success.

Being a kid is one of the most challenging times in life! But no matter what is happening in your life, and I mean NO MATTER WHAT, you can handle anything and move forward toward your dreams!

Look around you and make two lists: what are some good things in your life, and what are some things you'd like to change? Be honest with yourself. You can move to get around it once you see what is in your way.

For example, let's say someone is picking on you at school. He's older and bigger than you are, so there's nothing you can do about it. You just have to live with it. That wouldn't count as something you can change because you will never be able to.

Oh, really?

> "Success is the ability to go from one failure to another with no loss of enthusiasm."
> —Winston Churchill

If you see a problem and acknowledge it is there, you can find a way to change it. Say it. "That guy is a jerk to me, and I want him to leave me alone." Now you have something to work with! You have a goal to work towards.

How quickly can you change or get around a problem?

It depends on how big it is and how long it's been a problem. It might not happen in one day.

Every day, you get bigger, stronger, and hopefully smarter. Maybe you could find a friend with a similar problem, and together, you can develop a scheme to end it. Maybe you decide to take self-defense classes so that when you are a little older, you can tell him to stop and defend yourself physically if you need to.

Never let yourself think, "There is nothing I can do about this; I'll just need to learn to live with it."

There is ALWAYS something that can be done about it. Always 100% guaranteed. You can fix any problem in your life and have what you want. Don't ever forget this.

In Closing

> **"Learn to love the hate.**
> **Embrace it. Enjoy it. Everyone is entitled to their own opinion, and everyone should have one about you. Haters are a good problem to have. Nobody hates the good ones.**

They hate the great ones."

—**Kobe Bryant**

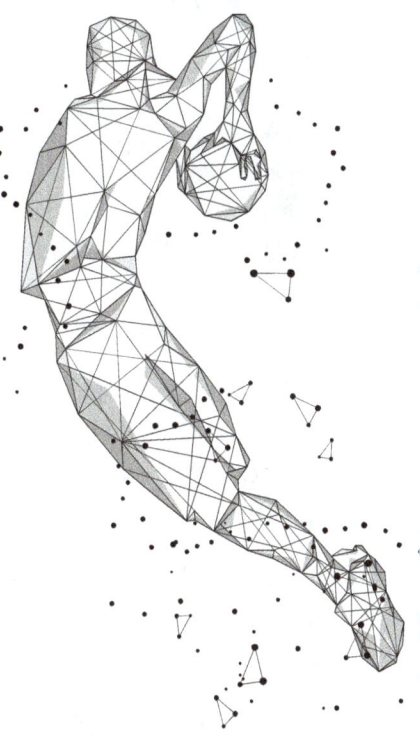

It takes time to achieve goals, change things you don't like, learn new things, and create new habits. Nothing worthwhile is easy, and nothing big arrives overnight. Pay attention to your actions every day. Ask yourself if your actions are helping your goal or not. If they are helping, keep doing them. If they are not helping, don't do them as much. And if they are pushing your goal farther away, stop them immediately! This also applies to the people you have in your life. People are good for you, or they are not. Figure out which and make sure you always have good people around you.

You are smart. I believe in you. You can accomplish anything you want in life.

> *If you hear a voice within you say "You cannot paint," then by all means paint and that voice will be silenced.*
> —Vincent Van Gogh

Anything. Believe it.

If this career doesn't feel right, no problem. Pick up another *Your Best Rockin' Life* book and learn about something else. You'll know the right path when you come across it. It will feel natural and easily fall into place.

Please call us if you need help with anything at all. Our #1 goal is for YOU to be successful and happy. We want to help, no matter what challenges you are facing.

Please send us your success stories, too! I love hearing if you enjoyed something or learned something that excites you. Please email me at denise@rockyourlifemedia.com.

I look forward to your success!!

All the very best,

GLOSSARY
Photographer

35mm Film – A type of film used for still photography. It came in a cylindrical cartridge and pictures were taken on it one after another, like a roll of tape. Also called 135 film. The number is for the size of the film, which was 35 millimeters. See the negative picture on page 41.

Aaron Siskind – He was an American photographer who lived from December 4, 1903, to February 8, 1991. He's known for his black-and-white, aerial and close-range photos of surfaces and objects.

Adaptable – Able to adjust oneself easily to different situations.

Advertising – The act of calling attention to a product or service with pictures, TV commercials, ads in magazines or in other ways. For example, some of the best creative advertising is shown in commercials during the Super Bowl.

Advertising professional – Someone who works with a client to determine to how best sell their product or service and then create plans and ads (print, radio, tv, internet, etc.) to sell it.

Aerial – In the air. A photographer that does aerial photography travels in planes, helicopters or uses drones to photograph landscapes, buildings or other things seen from the air.

Aesthetic – Relating to and involving emotion and sensation, as opposed to intelligence. Some would say this includes how appealing something is, as in beautiful or ugly.

Amateur – Someone who does something just for fun and doesn't plan to sell what they are doing. It could also be someone who is learning something, but before he fully knows how to do it.

Ambitious – having the quality of wanting to achieve your goals, and eager to do the work needed.

Anatomy – The science and study of the physical structure of living things, such a people, animals and plants.

Annie Liebovitz – An American portrait photographer of celebrities. She is known for her dramatic, quirky, and personal pictures and has been featured in many magazines such as Vanity Fair and Rolling Stone. She was born October 2nd, 1949.

Ansel Adams – An American landscape photographer who was best known for his black and white photographs, many of Yosemite National Park. He was born in 1902 and died in 1984.

Aperture – An opening, hole, or crack that only lets a limited light through it.

Appraiser – A person who's job it is to determine how much money something is worth, like a house or a car that was in an accident.

Apprentice – A person who works with and for another person to learn how to do a job or trade (a certain skill needed to do a job).

Architecture – The career of designing buildings and outside open areas for aesthetic (artistic) effect and often includes the decorations and furnishings.

Athletic trainer – A licensed health care professional that works with sports teams and athletes to train them physically.

Attorney – Also called a lawyer. Someone who practices law, to help his/her client in a legal case against someone else.

Auto Mechanic – A person whose job is to do repairs or other things to help keep cars working.

Glossary

Bachelor's Degree – A certificate of completion of 4-years worth of college classes. It's about 40 classes covering basic studies and also classes that focus on one area, such as business, arts, or science.

Blueprint – A reproduction (copy) of a technical drawing using a printing process on light sensitive paper. It allowed any number of copies of something to be created.

Brand – Something that communicates about a product or service. The Nike swish is one brand almost everyone knows.

Broadcast journalist – The person in the field of the news that "broadcasts" news via radio, television or videos, rather than older methods of communicating news, such as newspapers and printed ads.

Broadcasting – The business of radio or TV.

Business card – A small card one uses in business to provide his name, job title, company, address, email address and phone number. He gives this card to others so they have all the ways to reach him regarding business.

Business of Photography – The basics of running a photography business, including invoicing and budgeting, planning and operations and marketing.

Camera Operator – A professional that operates a film or video camera as part of a film crew. Also called cameraman – which is used whether the operator is a man or woman.

Candid – honest, open, informal. For example: She was very candid when she spoke about the accident.

Caterer – A person who makes a living providing food and drink for an event or gathering, at the location of the event.

Charming – Pleasing to others and delightful to have around.

Client – Also called customer. The person or company that buys the products or services of another.

Collodion Process – A photo developing process developed in 1851 by Frederick Scott Archer a year after it was explained by Gustave Le Gray. In the process, the photographic material (film) needs to be coated and prepared for light (sensitized), exposed to a certain amount of light, and developed in the space of fifteen minutes.

Commercial photographers – photographers that take photos of different subjects like buildings, merchandise, landscapes or other "things", usually for the purpose of advertising.

Complementary Colors – Colors that are opposite of each other on the color wheel, meaning if they are combined with each other they cancel each other to make black or white. Or, another way, it's a color that is the mixture of one primary color (red, yellow or blue) that is mixed with the color made of the other two primary colors combined. So, the complementary color of yellow would be purple (the combination of blue and red).

Composition – All the parts of what is needed for art (photography) to achieve a final picture that works.

Coroner – A person that works for a county or government office whose job it is to investigate and provide information about a death, especially if it doesn't appear the death was from natural causes.

Creative Eye – When you see something, it inspires you to create something from it, or to turn it into something artistic.

Cyan – The bluish color created from combining equal amount of light blue and green.

Design Technologist – A person who works with both the design and development teams for digital products, websites or web applications. Knowing graphic design and coding will help in this job.

Glossary

Diagnosis – In the medical field, examining symptoms to determine the cause of an illness to treat it.

Digital Design – Photography training that includes creating concepts and solving design problems to ensure photos communicate the intended message to the viewer.

DIY – Do It Yourself. In this case, determining on your own what education you need, as opposed to taking a curriculum at a school.

Documentary – Something related to an actual event, life story or specific time in history. A true story.

Don McCullin – A British Photojournalist known for his war photography and capturing images about people going through life struggles. He was born in 1935.

Drone – An aircraft device that is unmanned (doesn't have a person in it) but is controlled by someone using a remote control.

Efficient – Getting something done quickly and in the best possible way without wasting time; capable.

Elliott Erwitt – A French-born American photographer known for taking black and white pictures of funny everyday situations. He was born in 1928.

Empathetic – Understanding and courteous to the feelings, thoughts and attitudes of others.

Emulsion – a type of material made up from different silver chemicals that are suspended in a gelatin, and very sensitive to light. It's applied in a thin layer to a surface of film to allow a picture to be taken onto it.

Endeavor – To strive or move in the direction of achieving something.

Engineering – The art and science of construction of things such as engines, bridges, buildings, ships, etc.

Entry-level – This describes a job that requires minimal education, experience and training to start.

Escrow Officer – The person that helps organize and deliver all the documents and money between the buyer and seller in a real estate transaction.

Evidence – Something presented in a court case to prove the facts, such as records, documents, pictures or even statements by people who were there.

Exhibition – A display of artistic creations in a public place such as art gallery, museum or fair.

Exposure – The act of not covering it up but laying open and uncovered.

Film Editor – A person who manipulates film, taking out or piecing together to make a completed movie. He works with the cameraman and sound editors to bring sight, sound and vision together.

Filter – In photography, a tool used to make images look more vibrant and clear by cutting glare from shiny surfaces, darkening skies or reducing haze.

Fine-Arts photographers – photographers that take artistic photos and use creativity with their lighting or other equipment with the goal of selling the photos as art.

Flash Drive – Also called a USB flash drive is a data storage device that is removable from a computer or camera. Pictures can be put onto the drive and then removed to put onto another device, or to give as a digital portfolio.

Foundation – The basis or groundwork for any activity or structure.

Franchise – A license given to a person or group to market its products and services in a certain area. It could be a store or restaurant that is a national chain, like McDonald's, where one person owns all the McDonald's in his city. He has to follow all the rules of operating McDonald's so they are all run the same, but he could be the owner himself of one or more.

Freelance – A type of work where a person works for several people or companies, at different times and doing different projects. He can take clients or projects, or not take them, at his choice.

Fundamentals of Photography – A basic photography class that teaches basics such as using a digital camera, equipment, lighting and how to best create a picture.

G.I. Bill – A governmental program that provides financial assistance to military to use for college, vocational courses, job training or flight training.

Graduate School – A school that awards advanced degrees such as a master's degree (a "master" of a specific study or subject) or a doctorate, which means you have received such a high level of achievement in a field that you are able to teach it to others. Graduate school comes after "undergraduate school" where you would earn an associate's or bachelor's degree.

Grant – Money that is given without needing to be paid back. It's usually from a government, corporation or **foundation** for a person, school or **non-profit** business for reasons specified in the grant requirements.

Graphic designer – A person who designs text and pictures together for use in advertisements, magazines, books or other forms of communication.

Greg Gorman – An American portrait photographer born on November 30th, 1949 who is known for his intriguing photographs of celebrities in entertainment, sports, art, and music. He's also a sought after speaker in the photography community.

Headshots – A picture taken of a person's upper body or head, focusing on the face. They are taken for professional reasons, or to be used on social media, websites, business cards or other items to promote the person.

High Profile – Well-known or attracting special attention for something.

Human Resources – The person or department in a business that manages employees, from hiring and paying them, providing benefits, and managing their performance.

Humble – Not thinking of yourself as better than others; not pointing out your importance.

Imaging and Digital Processing – A photography class where students learn how to use digital software and the basics of digital color theory, file formats and photo editing.

Industrial Designer – This designer helps to develop designs for products we use, such as refrigerators, golf carts, or computers. It helps to know about art, graphic design, business and engineering to help them in the design process.

Industry standard – Something that is working in a specific area of business that the majority in that industry understand and are using.

In-State Tuition – The amount of money you pay to a college or university when you live in the state the school is in. You will typically pay a lot more to attend a college or university outside the state you live in.

Interest – Money paid to a lender, in addition to the loan amount, as a "thank you" for the loan.

Internet browser – A software program on a computer that allows you to view web pages on it. For example, if you open the Google browser and search "photographer", it will list lots of websites for that subject. You can click on whichever one you want and it will take you to that specific web page.

Glossary

Internship – It's a job a student takes to work in a company to learn and gain experience, or as a requirement to qualify for a job. It does not earn much money or is often done without pay.

Irving Penn – An American photographer known for his fashion photography, portraits and **still lifes**. Much of his fashion work was for Vogue magazine. He was born in 1917 and died in 2009.

Jim Marshall – Jim was an American photojournalist who lived from February 3, 1936 to March 24, 2010. He was known for his photographs of musicians in the 1960s and 1970s.

Kobe Bryant – An American professional basketball player who played for 20 years for the Los Angeles Lakers. He was regarded as the greatest basketball player of all time. He was born in 1978 and died in 2020.

Learn your trade – practice and do things that will make you better at the activities of your job, which is also called a trade.

Lens (for camera) – A piece of equipment that works with a camera used to bring or direct light to a specific fixed focal point for the purpose of taking a picture. There are different types of lenses for different types of photography, and some lenses work alongside other lenses.

Lighting Specialist – A person that works on a film set to install, test and change lighting as needed for the needs of the project.

Listing – A home or other property for sale or put on the "list" of properties for sale.

Logical – Putting together the pieces of something, or information, in a way that makes sense to others.

Machine operator – A person who operates a machine, or machinery for the company he works for, and many times requires a special operator's license. Examples of this are: operating a tractor, bulldozer or dump truck.

Magenta – The reddish color created from combining equal amounts of blue and red.

Major – The course of study to earn a bachelor's degree. If you want a degree in graphic design, Graphic Design would be your major. If you wanted to also learn art history, but didn't want to get a full bachelor's degree, you could "minor" in Art History, which would mean you take the required classes for art history to earn it as a minor.

Manual Camera – A camera that a photographer uses that allows him/her to adjust the exposure by choosing a **shutter speed** and **aperture** value.

Mark Twain – An American writer, publisher and lecturer who lived 1835-1910 and was known as the "greatest humorist the United States has produced" because of his humorous style of writing.

Marketing – Activities that are done by people or businesses to help buy or sell things.

Marketing professional – A person who works to create strategies and ideas to help businesses get more customers or clients.

Mechanical Film Camera – A camera that functions mechanically using photographic film, unlike a digital camera that functions with computer technology. A mechanical film camera has an actual shutter that opens and closes when a picture is taken.

Memory Card – A small, portable device containing memory to be used in a camera or cell phone when extra memory is needed.

Mentor – Someone who helps another by teaching him/her something, like how to get better at a skill or improve a talent.

Networking – People that have the same interest in something (like a career or industry) that talk and get together to see how they can help each other.

Niche – a specific place or position that is best or most appropriate for a person or thing. Specialty.

Non-Profit – A type of group or business that exists to help a cause, not make money.

Observant – Quick to notice things; being alert and aware of what's happening.

On the Job Training – Training you do while you are doing the job. As opposed to a school education, which you do before you start the job.

Open House – When a real estate agent puts out signs in the neighborhood with arrows pointing to the house and "opens" it up by inviting people inside the property to see if they want to buy it. An open house could be public (for anyone), or just for real estate professionals and usually lasts a few hours.

Pele – A famous Brazilian soccer player, born in 1940. It has been said that the was the greatest "footballer" of all time.

Perseverance – Continuing in a direction, without stopping at roadblocks.

Persuasive – Able to convince others about what you believe; getting them to agree with you or do something.

Photojournalist – a photographer that takes pictures of events, people and places for news outlets, magazines and TV.

Photo Shoot – A place where pictures are taken for a purpose, whether in a studio or outside (on location). All equipment, lighting and other photographic elements are in place to allow the photographer to take the picture needed.

Pixel – One small area of something that is displayed, usually on a computer. Many hundreds or thousands of these little pieces make up an image.

Portfolio – A collection of photos, art or other artistic creations that are kept in one place and used to showcase an artist's work. It can be in an actual book, or on a website.

Portrait photographer – A photographer that takes pictures of people. This could be someone that takes headshots (actor or business photos), photos of families, school pictures or sports.

Practical – Doing things in a way that makes sense, or is useful.

Premium – a higher price or cost than expected; superior.

Press Release – A written statement given by a company to the public that provides information about a topic related to that company that it wants others to know.

Procurement – Getting or obtaining something. If you are doing client procurement, you are doing activities that get people to be interested in your work enough to hire you.

Professional – Someone who does a job (as a profession, or career) to get paid.

Public relations executive – A person who works with businesses in helping and managing the communication between the business and its owners with the public and the media.

Public Speaking – Speaking in front of audiences, usually to teach them something or encourage them to do something.

Pun – using a word in a way that's different than expected, in a funny way. For example: The best way to communicate with a fish is to drop them a line. (You drop a fishing line into the water when you go fishing and there is a saying "drop me a line" when you want to communicate with someone.)

Referral – A person that recommends another person for something because they think that other person would do a good job.

Glossary

Resourceful – The ability to quickly adapt and deal with problems, new situations, etc.

Responsible – Being accountable for things around you in order to gain power or control over a situation.

Resume – A document about a person's work experience, including background, skills and accomplishments. Also called a CV, which means "curriculum vitae" – Latin for "the course of your life".

Retainer – Something (like money) given to hold for something else that will be coming later. For example, if you want to hire an attorney, you'll need to give him a retainer (or a set amount of money) in advance. As he works for you he will bill against (take) money from the retainer to pay for his services.

Retouching – To alter (change) a picture after it's taken to remove lines, lighten or correct.

Robert Adams – An American teacher of a Hindu spiritual practice known as Advaita. He was born in 1928 and died in 1997.

Salary – A fixed amount that is paid to someone for work over a certain period of time. A monthly salary, for example, would be a set amount to be paid for the month, no matter how much work is actually done.

Salesperson – A person who gets individuals or businesses to buy products or services from other individuals or businesses. Usually he earns a part of what he sells, called a commission.

Science – Knowledge that is gained by observation (looking at) and experimentation.

Scientific photographers – photographers that take pictures of things needed for scientific or medical work. They can take photos of things so small they can only be seen through a microscope.

Scholarship – An award of financial aid (money) to use for education. They are awarded based on criteria that is determined by the giver and does not need to be repaid. For example, someone could earn a scholarship because they are a gifted athlete or an exceptional student in some subject. There are many different kinds of scholarships given for as many different reasons.

Select – Those special photos the photographer chooses from a shoot that he or she believes are the exact type of picture their client wants.

Selfless – Not thinking about yourself but thinking of others instead; unselfish.

Self-sufficient – Able to take care of things yourself, without the help of others.

Shutter speed – The speed at which a "shutter" (kind of like a door) is opened in a camera to let light in to create a picture. The faster the speed, the more accurately and clearly it will capture the picture. The slower the speed, the less accurate and clear the picture will be.

Side Jobs – Work that someone does to earn extra money that is usually not full-time and is separate from their primary job.

Simon Sinek – A British/American author, motivational speaker and marketing consultant. He was born in 1973.

Sir John Herschel – An English mathematician, astronomer, chemist, inventor and photographer who invented the **blueprint**. He lived from 1792-1871.

Spontaneous – Having natural impulses to do things that are not planned.

Sports agent – A person who works with professional athletes and coaches to help them negotiate the contracts of their work, including who they will work for and for how long, how much money they will make and how much they will get paid for doing advertising for outside companies.

Sports medicine specialist – A person who is trained to provide medical care to athletes when they are injured. Some are doctors, and some are trained to do surgical procedures when needed.

Sports photographer – A photographer that works in the athletic industry. It's a branch of photojournalism that is specific to sports.

Steven Meisel – An American fashion photographer born on June 5, 1954, and known for his work in Vogue and Vogue Italia and his many pictures of celebrities.

Still life pictures – Pictures of objects, sometimes in small groups, showing it "still" in life.

Stock Photo Agency – An agency that buys many different kinds of photos, which they then try to sell. See www.stock.adobe.com for examples.

Stock Photographer – A photographer that takes photos that agencies are looking to "stock" for purchase. See www.stock.adobe.com for examples.

Student Loan – A loan taken out by a bank or other financial company to be used for school tuition, books, supplies and living expenses. It needs to be paid back, with *interest*.

Subtractive Color Image – The image created by mixing color filters and putting a white light on it from behind, allowing different colors to come forward.

Tenacity – the quality of being persistent, or not giving up on something you want.

Theory – A discussion or look into explaining something by comparing all the information about it, including facts.

Tinseltown – Another name for Hollywood, which is an area in Los Angeles, California.

Title document – The document that shows the owner of something. A chain of title shows all previous owners.

Title Rep – The person in a real estate transaction that assists the listing agent and seller with generating the title report and delivering it to the buyer.

Trade School – Also called a vocational school. A school you'd go to after high school to learn a trade (a certain skill needed to do a job) by taking classes only related to that trade. Some examples of trades would be dental assistant, forklift operator, plumber and carpenter.

Trend – Something that has become popular. "Wearing logo t-shirts has become a big trend among teens in the last few years."

Tripod – A three-legged stand used to support a camera.

Undergraduate Degree – A college or university where you would earn an associate's or bachelor's degree. This comes before one would attend graduate school.

Unexposed Film – Film is used in a camera that records pictures to film when it's exposed to light. Unexposed film has not been exposed to light so doesn't have a picture on it yet. Once it's "exposed" to light, a picture is recorded on the film.

Up-front – Paid or given in advance.

Vincent Van Gogh – A Dutch painter who lived from 1853 to 1890. He created about 2100 pieces of art, including 860 oil paintings. He became famous for his artwork after he died.

Virat Kohli – An Indian cricket (a bat and ball game played between two teams that each have eleven players on the field) player known as one of the best batsmen of his era. He was born in 1988.

Vocational – Related to a career or occupation (job). Comes from Latin 'vocatio' – a call or summons.

Wannabe – Want to be. "She's a wannabe rock star."

Winston Churchill – Prime Minister (elected head of the government) of the United Kingdom from 1940-1945.

Word-of-mouth – means something spoken from the mouth. Can be used as a form of advertising where people talk about their experiences to others, which causes others to take action (or not).

Work ethic – The time and effort one puts into his work. When one works hard, puts in extra time, and is dedicated and committed to his work, he is said to have a positive work ethic.

www.ingramcontent.com/pod-product-compliance
Lightning Source LLC
Chambersburg PA
CBHW060509030426
42337CB00015B/1810